THE PRATT LIBRARY ALBUM:
Baltimore Neighborhoods in Focus

Merry Christmas
Uncle Brothie &
Aunt Estelle.

With love from
Augie & Sandy

Copyright © 1986 by The Enoch Pratt Free Library

First published 1986 by The Enoch Pratt Free Library,
400 Cathedral Street, Baltimore, Maryland 21201

Library of Congress Cataloging-in-Publication Data:

Kelly, Jacques, 1950-
    The Pratt Library album.

    Includes index.
    1. Baltimore (Md.) — Description — Views. 2.
Baltimore (Md.) — Social life and customs — Pictorial
works. 3. Enoch Pratt Free Library — History —
Pictorial works. I. Enoch Pratt Free Library. II. Title.

F189.B143K45 1986   027.4752'6   86-11522

ISBN 0-910556-23-7

Cover photos: The Central Enoch Pratt
Free Library, photographed in 1933, is
flanked on the left and back cover by a
1930s view of Exeter Street in East Baltimore. On the right is a detail of Roland
Avenue and the Roland Park Water Tower,
also from the 1930s. It is reproduced on
page 183.

THE PRATT LIBRARY
ALBUM
BALTIMORE
NEIGHBORHOODS
IN FOCUS

by Jacques Kelly

Published by
THE ENOCH PRATT FREE LIBRARY
Baltimore, Maryland

Artist Edwin Tunis, who drew a number of maps for the Pratt Library in the 1930s, created one for Richard H. Hart's "Enoch Pratt, the Story of a Plain Man," published by the library in 1935.

The map locates Pratt's libraries, as well as the other beneficiaries of his philanthropy — the Cheltenham House of Reformation, the Maryland School for the Deaf at Frederick, the Moses Sheppard & Enoch Pratt Hospital, as well as the sources of the Pratt fortunes — the National Farmers' and Planters' Bank, the Maryland Steamboat Company, his steamers "Enoch Pratt," "Ida" and "Tivoli," his iron yards, as well as his Charles Street counting room and warehouse. There he began his business in horseshoes, iron products, nails and coal.

Enoch Pratt was an active member and trustee of the Unitarian Church, Charles and Franklin streets. After his marriage to Maria Louisa Hyde, he moved to Pleasant Street, at Courtland, a small street which was leveled about 1914 to construct the present St. Paul Place. By 1848 Pratt's ever-multiplying fortunes allowed him to build a new residence at Park Avenue and Monument Street, now a part of the Maryland Historical Society complex of structures.

In 1860 he was elected president of the Farmers' and Planters' National Bank. Some twelve years later he bought the controlling interest in the Maryland Steamboat Company. If extant today, it would be located at Harborplace's Light Street Pavilion. Malster's shipyard, in southeast Baltimore, built his "Enoch Pratt," which sailed the Chesapeake and its tributaries until 1919, long after its owner's death. The steamer "Ida" was named after his wife, who had that nickname. "Tivoli," his country estate east of Govans, christened another boat.

Pratt also had stock investments in the P.W. & B. Railroad — the Philadelphia, Wilmington and Baltimore, which would become known as the Pennsylvania Railroad. This rail company controlled the Northern Central, which ran its trains from Calvert Station, Calvert and Bath streets.

Enoch Pratt served as treasurer of the Peabody Institute and was a trustee of the Workingmen's Institute, a Canton reading room.

Enoch Pratt was buried on a hill at Green Mount Cemetery in 1896. The grave is marked with a Scottish granite monument.

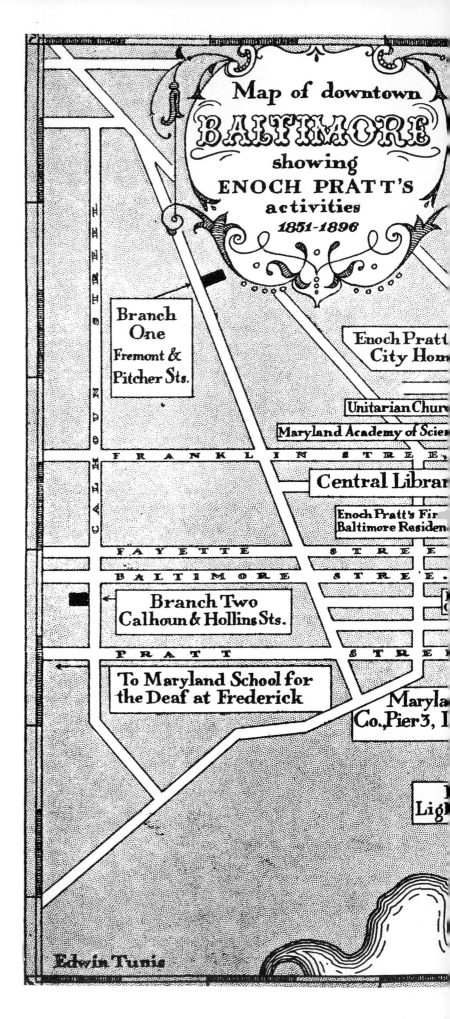

Map of downtown BALTIMORE showing ENOCH PRATT'S activities 1851-1896

Edwin Tunis

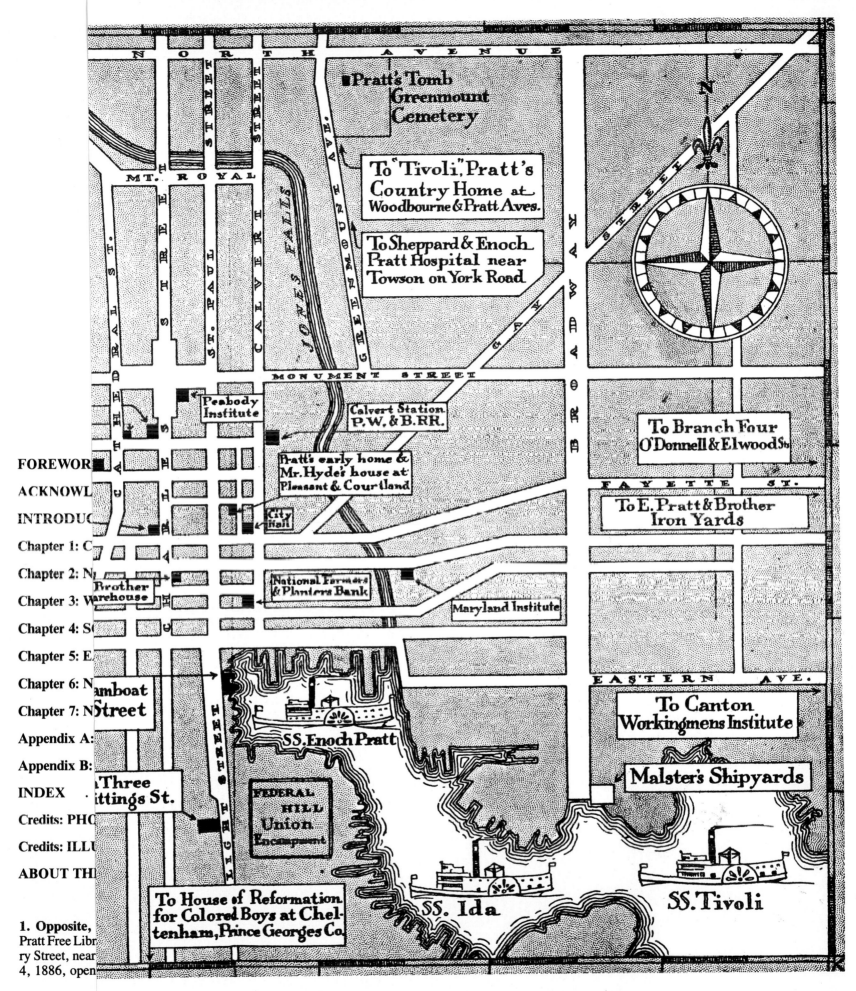

Pratt's Tomb
Greenmount
Cemetery

To "Tivoli", Pratt's
Country Home at
Woodbourne & Pratt Aves.

To Sheppard & Enoch
Pratt Hospital near
Towson on York Road

N

MONUMENT STREET

Peabody
Institute

Calvert Station.
P.W. & B.RR.

To Branch Four
O'Donnell & Elwood Sts.

Pratt's early home &
Mr. Hyde's house at
Pleasant & Courtland

FAYETTE ST.

To E. Pratt & Brother
Iron Yards

City
Hall

Brother
Warehouse

National Farmers
& Planters Bank

Maryland Institute

EASTERN AVE.

amboat
Street

To Canton
Workingmens Institute

SS. Enoch Pratt

Malster's Shipyards

Three
ittings St.

FEDERAL
HILL
Union
Encampment

To House of Reformation
for Colored Boys at Chel-
tenham, Prince Georges Co.

SS. Ida

SS. Tivoli

1. Opposite,
Pratt Free Libr
ry Street, near
4, 1886, open

v

FOREWORD

I first walked across the threshold of the world of magic embodied in the Pratt Library, in 1937. I was eleven years old, and recently moved from New Jersey to what seemed like a cold, alien, lonely city. Well, we must remember that eleven is a bad age to pull up human beings by their roots and transplant them to harsh climates. Though I much later came to love Baltimore and find that now it is a place that affords the landscapes for many of my best dreams, it seemed a bleak and cruel world when I was eleven, the new boy in the neighborhood and homesick for the place I'd left behind.

It was an uncle of mine, sensitive to the miseries that afflict small boys, who suggested I ought to drop in at the neighborhood library. I did. It was the branch at Hollins and Calhoun Streets, a dark brick structure in the style I think of as Victorian-Ecclesiastic, a whimsical little cathedral, as it were, to the printed word. What I recall most vividly was the sense of warmth that engulfed me as I entered the big room — it seemed vast at that time. Partly, I suppose, this was created by the dazzling colors — reds, blues and greens — that gleamed from the shelves where the books — there seemed to be thousands and thousands of books — were arrayed in their library bindings.

Mostly though, I suspect, the sense of warmth came from a child's instinctive realization that he had left a cold, cold world behind him and entered a realm where he could travel at will in exotic places with wonderful friends. There I experienced the broiling heat of India in company with ''King of the Khyber Rifles'' and adventured across Czarist Russia with ''Michael Strogoff.'' There, in that library, I passed some of the sweetest hours of my childhood, and saw places as amazing as any I have ever seen since, and met in those books people I shall never forget. The Pratt Library — a magical place of my childhood.

Russell Baker

3. Opposite, since 1933, Central's stately vestibule is a familiar sight to library patrons at 400 Cathedral Street. The public rooms are trimmed in tan marble, highlighted with black. Stylishly decorated brass was selected for the chandeliers, window screens, elevator surrounds and stair rails.

ACKNOWLEDGMENTS

The Pratt Library offered me a welcome assignment to produce a pictorial volume on its century of service to Baltimore and its neighborhoods. What better way to celebrate Pratt's role in this city than to illustrate it — the people and neighborhoods where Pratt has been a century-long friend? Any institution, represented in more than 30 neighborhoods, with a splendid and beloved downtown headquarters, was a logical focal point for toasting Baltimore, in all her alleys, brick houses, corner stores and library branches.

My work in culling the more interesting Baltimore neighborhood photographs was made easier by the help the Pratt and its ever-patient staff provided. Averil Kadis, the library's director of public relations, was an editor who steadfastly believed in the project from the beginning. Anna Curry, the Library Director, and Decatur Miller, President of the library's Board of Trustees, were enthusiastic proponents. Linda Lapides, Chair of the Centennial Task Force, made helpful suggestions, including the title.

Wesley Wilson and his Maryland Department librarians — Douglass Gray, Mary Catherine Kennedy, Jeff Korman and Eva Slezak, plus library staff members Bill Bond, Ralph Clayton, Mary Knauer and Barbara Waybright — offered and delivered assistance. Howard Hubbard and Sara L. Siebert generously offered their time and prolific memories.

Sandra R. Sparks, who designed the book, cared about each page, photograph and piece of type. Frederick Schwedes Jr. artfully facelifted the deteriorated photographs. The job of reading the manuscript went to James Hunt, Mike Giuliano and Earl Pruce.

Others deserve thanks: Muriel Ashley, Gerald Bordman, Earl Clayton, Allan Czarnowsky, James Dickson, Anne Erby, Richard Flint, Nancy Fenton, Michael Foreman, Michael Franch, Jeff Goldman, Clark Ickes, A. Michael Isekoff, James Kelmartin, June Kerr, Fred G. Kraft Jr., Dean Krimmel, Peter Liebhold, Mary Mannix, Emma Mitchell, Francis O'Connor, Eleanor Pape, Richard Parsons, Anita Prewitt, Mark Reeve, Fred Shoken, Marcy Silver, Robert Skillman, George Voith and Maurice Wells.

I also thank my parents, Stewart and Joseph Kelly, both of them prolific readers, who directed a curious son to the Pratt Library.

Jacques Kelly
March 31, 1986

4. Opposite, Depression-era readers use the new library building, built and fixtured for about $2.2 million, one-fifth less than the original estimate.

INTRODUCTION

A century ago, Enoch Pratt gave the citizens of Baltimore a free public library. He stipulated that the library was to be "for all, rich and poor, without distinction of race or color." Today the Enoch Pratt Free Library is a living testament to the vision of its founder and to the strong belief in the worth of freedom of inquiry, the preservation of knowledge, and the dissemination of information held by generations of Baltimoreans.

Included among the countless thousands who have have been beneficiaries of the legacy of Enoch Pratt is this grateful Baltimorean for whom the Pratt Library has been a lifelong source of learning, enrichment and inspiration. In progressing from preschooler excited by her first library card to Library Director confronted with the challenges of administration, my delight in the wonder and mysticism of this institution has never diminished.

Published in celebration of the Library's Centenary, this book is an expression in pictures and words of the role the Pratt Library has played, and continues to play, in Baltimore's diverse communities, sharing people's lives, stimulating their minds, shaping their dreams — partners in progress.

A single century, however, is but a beginning. With the trust and support of the citizenry it serves, the Enoch Pratt Free Library looks ahead to new centuries of challenge and achievement, enriching future generations with the wealth of resources for learning, information, and recreation best provided by a flourishing public library system.

Anna Curry
Director

5. Opposite, the serene Central opened February 3, 1933, about the time this photo was taken. The first floor has a naturally lighted main court which is surrounded by subject departments. The original furnishings and bookshelves were made of handsome walnut, while the high ceilings imparted an air of spacious seriousness.

6. When the old Central was constructed in the 1880s, it was considered up-to-date. But within 20 years it was being criticized as "crusty with architectural excesses on the outside and heavy with solemn gloom and inconvenience within." Few volumes were stored on open shelves. Pages called "slip chasers" hunted from attic to cellar for the book requested from this main circulation desk in 1920.

7. This behind-the-scenes cataloging room photo is from the 1890s. Note women working with gas-lighted lamps. The place bristled with signs and rules, such as: "Gentlemen will not wear their hats in any part of the library." In 1929, librarians experimented with pedometers to record their daily walking on stairs and corridors. The circulation desk's staff tallied four miles; the reference department, two miles. Old Central was designed by architect Charles L. Carson, who also drew plans for the first six branches. A curious public filled the reading room on Central's first day of regular service, January 5, 1886. Readers passed through the dark halls until December 1930, when books were moved to the Rouse Building, Hopkins Place and Redwood Street, while a new Central was being constructed. There was no interruption in service, however.

8. From the first, the Pratt book collections had a rather academic and serious tone. Lewis Steiner, the first librarian, was succeeded by his son, Bernard Christian Steiner. Both were scholarly and felt Baltimoreans were not well-served by cheap but popular novels. This 1890s view shows books being prepared for use.

9. Old Central's reading room was designed to hold 150 periodicals and newspapers, but contained only minor provision for a reference department. In 1925, H.L. Mencken came out for a new library, while blasting the antiquated building as "so infernally hideous that it ought to be pulled down by the common hangman. Nothing more dreadful was built in Baltimore during the awful eighties. The only thing that may be said in favor of it is that it is in a narrow street and is thus not too brilliantly visible." He suggested its Victorian facade "be torn off and thrown into the harbor . . . along with the bones of the architect who designed it."

10. As early as 1913, Pratt was acquiring old 400 block of Cathedral Street homes for library expansion. In November 1916, this photo's date, a children's department was opened in an adjacent house at Cathedral and Mulberry streets. Momentum for a modern Central library was growing during this period, but available funds went into neighborhood branch construction. The dynamic Joseph L. Wheeler (1884-1970) assumed duties as library director on July 1, 1926, and immediately overcame years of inertia. He and architect Alfred Morton Githens designed a new central library that learned by, and corrected, the mistakes of Victorian-era libraries.

12. Pratt's Central Library, 400 Cathedral Street, appeared resplendent as it opened in February 1933. Writer R.P. Harriss recalled that period: "I . . . remember the great surge of pride we all felt when it moved to its big Central building." Central was immediately hailed for its design and efficiency. The facade was lined with beckoning, department-store like windows, then as now filled with colorful displays. There were no steps to discourage entering patrons. It faces architect Benjamin H. Latrobe's Basilica of the Assumption.

13. When the new Central opened, children had their own fieldstone garden entrance along the building's Mulberry Street side. The Children's Department was one of Central's glories. Its ceiling was painted with colorful scenes from "Alice in Wonderland." Many Baltimoreans were introduced to a life of public library use through this gracious entrance.

11. **Opposite,** Baltimore's Mayor Howard Jackson, presided January 12, 1932 at cornerstone laying ceremonies for the new Pratt Central Library. The building was completed within 14 months.

15. A gracefully designed metal screen was set into the arch stretching atop Central's main entrance. Its tracery effect has delighted photographers since 1933, when this photograph was taken. Writer John Goodspeed said of the Pratt: "I regard the library as one of the true marks of civilization in a city that doesn't have as many as it pretends."

16. Central's main hall held the card catalog, which was housed in numerous wooden units. This 1935 photo shows a Pratt staff member at the information desk.

14. Opposite, Central's main court, 1933.

17. The Wheeler philosophy of pleasing library patrons is evident here in this 1936 photograph of the Edgar Allan Poe Room, one of the open-to-the-public sanctuaries within the Central Library. It featured leather-covered chairs, walnut-paneled walls, Oriental carpets, and a stenciled ceiling. This quiet retreat easily could have been mistaken for the reading room of a gentleman's club. Artist Thomas Corner donated the Poe portrait. The room was used for the popular "Afternoons with the Poets" series.

18. Central's Reference Department was designed with a fancy coffered ceiling.

19. Opposite, the cataloging room in the 1930s was a model of orderly production.

20. Opposite, the newspaper room in the middle 1930s seems a male domain. One patron reads **The Country Gentleman.** In 1985, film maker John Waters said of the Pratt's newspaper collections: "I have spent many hours poring over back issues, researching all the horrible things that have happened over this great nation. I've followed the trials and tribulations of the Manson family for the last 15 years in your library. I also like the really spooky people that seem to hang out in this section."

21. Thousands of Baltimore children received their first introduction to Pratt Central through the Children's Department and story-telling hours. This Pratt tradition began in 1927. Here an animated Marion Fiery sits before a young audience on December 29, 1933. When a fire in the massive hearth was lighted, the dragons' eyes on the fireplace screen glowed.

22. In the 1930s the Pratt told its story via its book delivery truck, which made daily rounds to neighborhood branches with books from the Central collection. In the background is Franklin Street and the old Catholic Daughters of America hall.

23. When Stewart & Company enlarged its Howard and Lexington streets department store, thousands of curious shoppers inspected the place September 22, 1913. The shoppers found a new soda fountain, 500-seat restaurant with a separate men's seating and smoking area and a new parcel delivery chute. Lace curtains were 49 cents a pair, portieres, 98 cents, and a man's suit, $12.50.

Chapter 1: **CENTRAL**

24. Opposite, Lexington Street shoppers huddle around the display in the May Company's window in December 1949. Window shopping was then a favorite downtown pastime. Many Baltimore families would finish their Thanksgiving Day meals then head downtown to stroll past the holiday lights and decorated windows. Merchants competed for artful displays of merchandise.

25. Central Pratt's windows have enticed readers since 1933. This 1961 display features an H.L. Mencken bibliography published by the library. Writer William Manchester recalled a 1940s incident about Mencken and the Pratt: "He was very proud of 'his library.' At that time the Mencken collection was not housed in a separate room; it was in a locked stack in the basement. Richard Hart gave Mencken the key and down we went. In unlocking the stack, Mencken somehow managed to twist the chain around his ovoid torso and lock himself to the steel grill."

26. Hopper-McGaw's window, Charles and Mulberry streets, featured Webster's cigars in 1923. The store, which operated from 1880 to 1957, featured fancy-food delicacies, wines and liquors. Tobaccos were stored in moist underground humidors. The store did its own baking and had a soda fountain and luncheonette. A wooden cigar-store Indian stood by the front door.

27. Pratt's first bookmobile was into its second month of service in February 1949 and attracted shoppers' attention on Lexington Street.

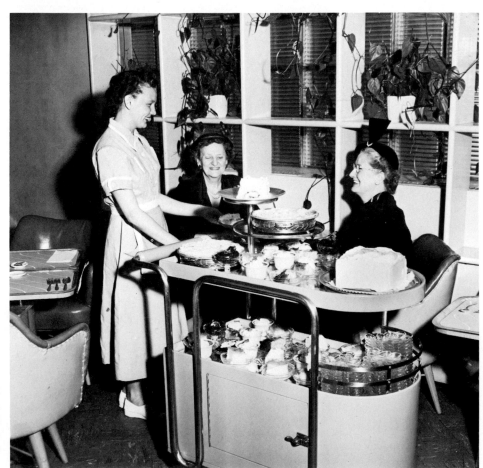

28. A favorite downtown lunching spot was the Quixie Restaurant on the sixth floor of the Hutzler Brothers department store. Two shoppers make a selection from the dessert cart in the early 1950s. The restaurant closed in 1972.

29. Easter shoppers pass corsage and candy egg stands outside Lexington Market in April 1939.

30. Smith's Book Store, 805 N. Howard Street, was a Baltimore institution founded in the 1870s. It once held 150,000 volumes. This favorite haunt of local bibliophiles closed in 1965.

31. Huyler's, at 14 W. Lexington Street, was famous for its chocolate candy, sundaes and light refreshments. The shop had a soda fountain in the front and table service in the rear. Founded in 1881, Huyler's was part of a national chain which flourished until 1951. Proximity to Lexington Street's Century and Valencia theaters did not hurt the chocolate-soda patronage, either.

33. **Opposite,** a busy May morning at Lexington and Eutaw Streets, 1946, at the Lexington Market's outdoor stalls. Novelist Christopher Morley described the market as that ''dear old parallelogram of plethora. . . . Here an aristocracy of good digestion shopped for victuals, choosing shad or birds or berries as a bibliophile would scrutinize first editions.''

32. Wartime shortages forced Baltimore housewives to wait for scarce chicken on April 15, 1945, on Lexington Street just west of Liberty Street. Lexington Street, with its movie theaters, dime and shoe stores, always seemed to be busy.

6

34. The 200 block of W. Biddle Street had fallen upon hard times in the middle 1930s. The early 19th-century homes still had their architectural integrity. The placards advertise Gwynn Oak Park, the popular Northwest Baltimore amusement park. H.L. Mencken wrote of Baltimore's rowhouse tradition in 1927: "The builders . . . were not given to useless ornamentation; their houses were plain in

design, and restful to the eye. A long row of them, to be sure, was somewhat monotonous, but it at least escaped being trashy and annoying.'' These homes were later demolished.

35. Maryland Institute students sketched and painted just outside Corpus Christi Church, Mount Royal Avenue, in the 1920s.

36. Large apartment houses often had dining rooms. The Marlborough, on Eutaw Place, featured this ''cafe'' in 1912. Note the water bottles on each crisply draped table. The Marlborough apartments possessed Old World elegance — French doors, high ceilings, marble fireplaces and brass light fixtures. The art-collecting Cone sisters were its most famous residents. Their apartments were filled with works by Matisse, Picasso and Cezanne, among other artists. The Marlborough still stands, thought its interior has been considerably altered.

37. Opposite, Bolton Street is filled with music, children's rides, crab soup, lemon sticks and people for an October 1974 Bolton Hill festival. Many of the neighborhood's Victorian homes had been restored in the previous decade. The community's name was suggested by Bolton, a stately house that stood for many years on the site of the Fifth Regiment Armory.

38. Mount Royal Station's expansive train shed welcomed passengers beginning September 1, 1896. Coal-burning steam locomotives were pulled into the station by smaller electric motor units to cut down on smoke in the Howard Street tunnel. In January 1899, the "Book of the Royal Blue" said, "This magnificent railway station was erected by the Baltimore and Ohio for the convenience of North

Baltimore residents, being about a mile and a half from Camden Station, the original railway station of the B&O in the southern part of town. The two stations are connected by the famous double-track tunnel, under the city, which is lighted by electricity and through which the trains are propelled by the same wonderful force.'' The station is now owned and used by the Maryland Institute.

39. The camera looks south along St. Paul and Charles streets from the top of the St. Paul Street Bridge just east of Pennsylvania Station, in 1920. Visible at left is the steeple of Christ Episcopal Church. Next to it are the Eleven East Chase building, Hotel Belvedere, First Presbyterian Church and Hotel Arundel. The benches in the terraced garden along Mount Royal Avenue were a vantage spot for

watching train movements. Mount Royal Avenue was lined with automobile showrooms where Baltimoreans bought Columbias, Briscoes, Peerless and Chalmers cars. The station was built in 1911 and replaced an earlier structure.

40. Standard Oil Company had a new service station at Maryland Avenue and Falls Road in March 1927. That same year H.L. Mencken wrote, ". . . the automobile men . . . seem to be quite unable to touch anything without making it ugly. . . . Wherever they set up one of their abominable gas cathedrals, the whole neighborhood is ruined."

42. Opposite, Pennsylvania Station's platform was filled with servicemen and other passengers on Labor Day, 1945. World War II made Baltimore a boom town and its train stations were always busy. Originally called Union Station, the station was built in 1911 with three stained glass circular rotunda windows, marble-clad walls, oak benches, brass lighting standards and Rookwood tile decorations. It was restored in 1980-1982.

41. New billboard advertising went up along Charles Street above Lafayette in July 1920. The signs did not please everyone, including H.L. Mencken, who wrote of this neighborhood in 1927, "What impression of the town does a stranger get when he first sees it from Union (Pennsylvania) Station? Here is a region in which millions have been spent for public improvements, but all that shows for the money is a series of glaring and preposterous signs. The effect is that of a third-rate street carnival. Baltimore looks cheap and silly."

43. The Meyer Davis Orchestra played at the Tent, a night club atop the roof of the Lyceum Theater in the 1200 block of N. Charles Street, in November 1924. The musicians included Nathan Brusiloff, Harry Campbell, Jack Scherr, Ray Welsh, Nicholas Vita, Howard Dolan and Stuart G. Whitmarsh. The Tent was a popular Prohibition-era club patronized by Baltimore socialites. The Davis orchestra went on to practically patent a distinctive "society beat" for fox trots at debutante parties across the country. The orchestra was regularly called up to play at presidential inaugural balls. Meyer Davis himself was born in Ellicott City.

44. The camera looks south on Charles Street at Lafayette Avenue, June 6, 1950, a period when Baltimore's streetcar network was being converted to bus operation. The Famous Ballroom featured "friendship dances" on Wednesdays, Fridays, Saturdays and Sundays. "Killer Shark" played the Times (now Charles) Theatre.

45. A new model General taxicab poses on East Mount Vernon Place, April 26, 1932. Behind the vehicle is the George Peabody statue. Peabody tapped Enoch Pratt to serve on the board of his Peabody Institute. Mount Vernon Place was conceived by the heirs of landowner and Revolutionary War figure John Eager Howard. They created four rectangles of land around the Washington Monument and then sold building lots for fine residences. By the 1860s gracious residences lined the square.

46. An Amoco service station, St. Paul Street and Mount Royal Avenue, served the Mount Vernon neighborhood in September 1935.

47. A No. 17 streetcar pauses briefly before crossing Mount Royal Avenue at Charles Street in March 1927. The trolley is bound for Camden Station, though it has just passed Pennsylvania Station. At the right is a Studebaker agency.

48. The Fifth Regiment marches across Madison Street at Howard in the early 1920s. The neighborhood has turned out for the event.

49. Writer William Stump described the Maryland Club, 1 East Eager Street, on its 100th anniversary (1957) as being: "free of pretense and chrome and canned music and urgency. . . ." The photo was shot in December 1922.

50. Beauty contestants line up outside the Hotel Stafford, Washington Place, in the Woodrow Wilson era.

51. The 1903 Hotel Belvedere, Charles and Chase streets, reopened the John Eager Howard Room in 1936. Artist O. Verna Rogers did the murals from prints of old Baltimore. The Hammond organ provided dance music.

52. A 1936 Metropolitan Opera performance at the Lyric draws a smartly dressed society crowd. Originally named the Music Hall, the auditorium opened with a gala Boston Symphony Orchestra performance October 31, 1894. Nellie Melba was the soloist. Over the years many musical legends performed here — Enrico Caruso, Geraldine Farrar, John McCormack, Giovanni Martinelli and Kirsten Flagstad. The Chicago and Metropolitan opera companies made regular annual visits to the Lyric, which was also the birthplace, in 1916, of the Baltimore Symphony Orchestra.

54. The Women's Civic League's Flower Mart arrives at Mount Vernon Place each spring, the first Wednesday in May. A photographer caught the 1936 version in the morning hours before the crowd had time to gather.

55. Easter Sunday worshippers leave Mount Vernon Place Methodist Church in in the 1940s. The church's masonry Gothic walls and steeple have a greenish cast to them. Architect Thomas Dixon had the local stone quarried at Bare Hills in Baltimore County. The church was dedicated November 21, 1872.

53. Opposite, the window of MacGillivray's drug store, Charles and Read streets, featured Palmolive soap — one free bottle of Palmolive shampoo with the purchase of six cakes of soap — in the early 1920s.

JULY-7-14.

56. Much fine federal architecture was destroyed when blocks of Franklin Street and other neighboring thoroughfares were condemned

and razed for the construction of St. Paul Place. This photo was taken July 7, 1914, just before demolition began.

58. Of all the Central Library's architectural wonders, the Children's Department's fish pond is vividly remembered by young library patrons. Here story-hour specialist Beth Caples leads a 1950s school-class visit to the miniature lagoon.

59. Central Library was filled with listeners for a series of atomic energy talks in 1947. Some 7,000 persons attended lectures and viewed displays.

57. Opposite, tree trimmers operate on a surviving Revolutionary War-era tree on the grounds of the Basilica of the Assumption at Charles and Mulberry streets, February 6, 1958.

60. Between the World Wars, Charles Street had it own fleet of double-decker buses. Novelist F. Scott Fitzgerald used his impressions of a ride on one for his 1936 short story, ''The Afternoon of an Author.''

61. Baltimore police inspect new equipment outside the old Fallsway headquarters in the 1930s.

62. Opposite, trolley passengers board a No. 15 Overlea-bound car in the middle 1920s on West Baltimore Street, near Hopkins Place.

63. Druid Hill Park is Baltimore's largest 19th century public park. Ice skaters took to its boat lake, February 10, 1934. In the warm weather months small boats were rented here. The shallow lake was also used as a goldfish hatchery for the city's public ponds and ornamental fountains. The Victorian house was known as the Island Lodge.

Chapter 2: **NORTHWEST**

64. In 1909, the 2000 block of Mount Royal Terrace, just above North Avenue, faced the circular reservoir built in 1861 which lent its name to the Reservoir Hill neighborhood. To the right is the Druid Apartment house, formerly a bicycling club. Residents liked to look at the water's surface from their second- and third-floor windows. The city discontinued using the reservoir in 1910, filled it, then seeded and planted it. Most of this was cut away for Jones Falls Expressway construction in the late 1950s.

65. A Studebaker climbs a steep Druid Hill Park hill, September 11, 1919.

66. This July 1915 view looks across Druid Lake to newly constructed Reservoir Hill mansions and apartments.

67. In the 1880s and 1890s, the bicycling craze hit Baltimore. This group of dignified cyclists posed for the camera on July 4, 1896 in Druid Hill Park.

68. Baltimore families loved Druid Hill Park's cool groves for picnics, as this July 1915 photograph shows. The park was established in 1860 and paid for by a penny tax levied on all horsecar passengers. Throughout the park were natural springs, a zoo, bandstand, pavilions, lakes, walks, promenades and statuary. On sweltering summer nights, Baltimoreans sought relief by sleeping in the park. Beginning in 1879, the park even had its own herd of sheep that cut down on the grass-cutting chores. The excess buck lambs brought $25.

69. Pratt's Branch 1, shown here in 1895, was located at Fremont Avenue and Pitcher Street. It opened March 15, 1886 and was one of the first four Pratt neighborhood branches. It closed in 1957 following the opening of a new streamlined branch at Pennsylvania and North avenues.

70. Branch 1 in the late 1940s. By this time, the building was more than 55 years old and showing signs of hard usage. The building was also involved in an early civil rights suit. Louise Kerr, a black Baltimore elementary school teacher, sued the library for admission to its librarians' training class. Pratt trustees said there was no librarian's vacancy in Branch 1, the branch mainly used by black Baltimoreans. The U.S. Court of Appeals heard the case, declared the Pratt a public institution and decided in favor of Miss Kerr.

71. Opposite, Martha M. Brown, a resident of the 1000 block of Arlington Avenue, has just left Pratt's Branch 1, Fremont Avenue and Pitcher Street, October 18, 1907. The sidewalks were then brick-paved and the gutters laid in rubble stone.

72. In the early 1950s, a Mosher Street cab crosses Pennsylvania Avenue, the city's major black entertainment-shopping district.

73. Just about any magazine or newspaper could be bought at North and Linden avenues in the late 1940s. The city was then more densely populated. Busy pedestrian activity was then a common sight. Nearby was Nate's and Leon's, the delicatessen restaurant that stayed open long hours and attracted show people, politicians and countless less well known customers.

74. J.J. Brill's market, in the 1800 block of Pennsylvania Avenue, was picketed in June and July 1971. Several groups, including the Black Panthers, had organized a boycott. The groups wanted money for a day care center and food program. A city judge stopped the picketing July 9, 1971.

75. The always busy crosstown No. 13 streetcar stops for a passenger at North and Pennsylvania avenues in the early 1920s. The William J. Tickner & Sons funeral parlor was once one of the largest undertaking businesses in the city.

76. A Northwest Baltimore street artist displays his works in 1948.

77. Opposite, C. E. Haen, a Northwest Baltimore resident, returns home from a morning's shopping at Lafayette Market January 14, 1904. She is entering a wooden back gate, part of the high wood fences that were common to rowhouse back yards. Note the fish and produce hanging from her market basket. The market is located at Pennsylvania Avenue and Laurens Street.

78. First Lady Eleanor Roosevelt visited Douglass High School in December, 1935. She gave a speech and was presented with a floral bouquet. This school building, which opened in 1925, was located at Carey, Baker and Calhoun streets. The school was founded in 1883 and had several earlier locations, including one at Pennsylvania Avenue and Dolphin Street. It was the state's first senior high school erected for blacks. It moved to Gwynns Falls Parkway in 1954.

79. The corner of Madison Avenue and Dolphin Street in the late 1920s was a busy streetcar transfer point.

80. This August 27, 1925 view of the 900 block of Druid Hill Avenue looks north toward tiny Numsen Street.

81. The built-up city was beginning to encroach upon estates and undeveloped land about 1910. Here is the 2300 block Reisterstown Road, with the houses on the left situated between Ruskin and Orem avenues. They face the lawns of the Mondawmin estate, left. The streetcar tracks continue on out Reisterstown Road. The street sign indicates Elgin Avenue.

82. The 2100 block of Etting Street, between Bloom and Gold streets, 1937, was typical of Baltimore's hundreds of small streets lined with red brick, two-story rowhouses. This block is particularly well maintained. The white-painted wooden steps and sidewalk decorations bespeak the residents' pride in their block, which was then lighted by a gas street lamp.

83. Gas lights, but no trees, have been placed on Gwynns Falls Parkway at Longwood Street, looking west in the 1920s. Baltimore's system of tree-lined parkways was designed by the Olmsted Brothers, the pioneering landscape architecture firm. This boulevard was envisioned to connect Gwynns Falls Park with Druid Hill Park using a strip of green grass and trees. The Highland Park Hotel, an 1870s Victorian summer residence, was once located just north of this spot.

84. Members of the Fortnightly Club, hosted by Mrs. Howard W. Jackson, left, 2402 Talbot Road, Windsor Hills, enjoy lemonade outdoors. Mrs. William J. Brown is in the center and Mrs. J. Hughes Murphy is on the right, June 6, 1937.

85. Opposite, on a June 1925 day, students enrolled in Marjorie Martinet's painting school visited the unpaved streets of the paper and textile mill village then called Hillsdale, but best known as Dickeyville. The entire community was in a state of decay when it was auctioned off in November, 1934 for $42,000. Its homes were subsequently restored

86. The Pratt's old Walbrook Branch, No. 8, Bloomingdale Road and Clifton Avenue, was donated to the library by real estate developer Francis White. It had been a Presbyterian church before its conversion to a library in September 1907. But many people still confused the building with a church. In 1943, members of the Temple Baptist Church took up a collection and bought the Pratt an electric sign to end the decades of confusion.

87. The Pratt began delivering lots of 200 books to Walbrook, the early Northwest Baltimore suburb, in 1899. Demand was high. The first library station was a school room. A converted trolley waiting shed followed. In September 1907 this old wooden church was donated and a permanent library branch, No. 8, established. Only religious fixtures were removed and the library's shelves, desks and books added. The building experienced heavy use for the next 50 years and was replaced by a new structure in 1957.

88. Prior to World War II, Baltimoreans traveled by streetcar. Here, at the intersection of Liberty Heights Avenue and Reisterstown Road, February 6, 1932, car tracks branched off to serve different neighborhoods. To the right is Druid Hill Park.

89. Buddy Deane, shown here in June 1960 during a television strike, was voted America's No. 1 disc jockey in 1962. His "Buddy Deane Show" aired on Channel 13, Television Hill, from 1957 to 1964.

90. Opposite, Elementary School 59, the Louisa May Alcott School, at Reisterstown Road and Keyworth Avenue, was built in 1910 and known for its motivated students and active parents' association. The photo was taken in 1930, when the Pratt Library was delivering weekly "classroom collections" because the school had no library. Each group of 30-40 books was housed in a substantial wood box with a door and placed in a classroom for teachers to use with their students. The books were tantalizing samples of what waited for students at the nearby Keyworth Avenue Pratt branch.

92. In 1947 a No. 33 streetcar has left West Arlington and heads downtown at Park Circle, just opposite the entrance to Carlin's Park. A large sign proclaims Gunther's beer atop Leon Lapides' delicatessen. Streetcars disappeared from Northwest Baltimore in the 1950s.

93. Carlin's Park's prime location on several streetcar lines gave it citywide drawing power. This 1920 photo of a pavilion decorated in a circus motif gives an indication of the park's inventory. The fireworks display on July 4, 1920 was designed to resemble "the bombardment of Verdun."

91. Opposite, a performance of "Cavaliera Rusticana," July 23, 1921, at Carlin's Park, Park Circle, filled the open-air stands. John J. Carlin opened his 70-acre amusement park shortly after World War I on part of the Gittings family's Ashburton tract. The park became best known not for opera, but for its Rocky Mountain Speedway, dances, swimming pool and ice rink. The park lasted until the early 1960s.

94. An April 1948 streetcar and auto accident in the 4300 block Park Heights Avenue drew considerable neighborhood attention. The

54

car's driver was not injured, but the event provided enough neighborhood drama to interrupt business.

95. The Read Drug and Chemical Company was Baltimore's largest chain, where customers enjoyed their lemon phosphates made at soda fountains. Shown here September 6, 1932, is the unit at Park Heights and Belvedere avenues, when "Run Right to Read's" was a

56

well known Baltimore promotional slogan. This Read's was one of the busiest in the chain. Its soda fountain offered Hendler's ice cream while its patent medicine counters held scores of locally famous remedies such as Bromo-Seltzer and Dr. Gordschell's salve.

96. Mount Washington had its own airport, the Curtiss Wright Field. In August, 1940, a group of University of Baltimore students inspect a Curtiss dive bomber. Included were Robert Boyle, Norman Waltjen, Henri Lederer, Jerry Hege, Frank Brown, Richard Price, Lieut. Thomas W. Wagner, Edward M. Volz, Chapman Reed, John Watkins and Edward Kohn.

97. One of the most noted match races in sporting history was staged at Pimlico November 1, 1938. Jockey Georgie Woolf rode Seabiscuit to a decisive victory over War Admiral in this two-horse contest called the "Pimlico Special." Woolf often referred to Seabiscuit as "the greatest horse I ever rode."

98. Real estate developers Webb and White promoted and sold a section of Mount Washington as Hill Top Park, the area crossed by Arden, Oakshire, Crest and Ridgedale roads and Cross Country Boulevard. Hill Top referred to "Old Hilltop," the popular name given Pimlico race course. This May 11, 1913 photograph shows one of the newest Hill Top Park shingled homes. The Pratt Library's 1913 annual report noted a drop in summer book circulation figures in Northwest Baltimore. It stated, "People in semi-suburban sections like this live principally out-of-doors and on their porches in the warm weather and do not care for the exertion of reading."

99. In 1936, one of these new Homer Avenue homes, off the 4400 block of Reisterstown Road, sold for $4,300 and up. Built by William French, they featured hot water heat, oak floors, a masonry garage, tiled porches and Real Host kitchen ranges.

100. Popular entertainer Sophie Tucker makes a visit to the Levindale home for the aged in March, 1934.

101. The 3800 block of Liberty Heights Avenue, at Garrison Boulevard, May 9, 1937. Represented were an American grocery store, Arundel ice cream, Fish cleaning, Michael Weiss jewelers, the Harris delicatessen, Simon Malkin hardware and Lambros Brothers.

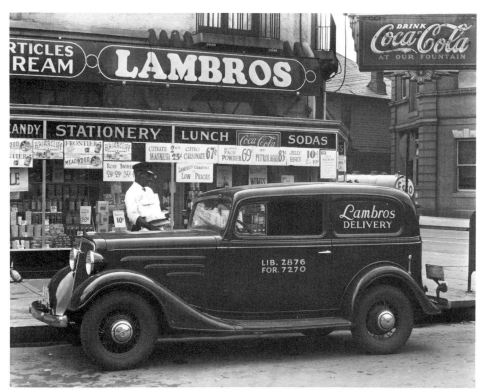

102. Lambros Brothers' delivery truck is ready to carry customers' purchases home on April 6, 1935, at Liberty Heights Avenue and Garrison Boulevard.

103. The Ambassador Theater, Liberty Heights and Gwynn Oak avenues, featured Paul Muni and Ann Dvorak in "Dr. Socrates" in 1935. Neon lights ablaze, the art deco-style film house opened September 18 of that year. The Ambassador had its own liveried doorman.

104. Trees shade the comfortable office of Dr. A. Clarence Smink, 4509 Liberty Heights Avenue on October. 1, 1937.

105. The Mordecai Gist school, No. 69, Granada and Oakford avenues, West Arlington, was photographed February 11, 1931. The West Arlington water tower, which once supplied this neighborhood, is in the background. West Arlington was one of the city's older residential suburbs. It was initially developed in the 1890s.

106. An October 18, 1948 rally of workers at the Baltimore and Ohio Railroad's Mt. Clare shops celebrated the completion of the fortieth mountain-type locomotive, a project that began in 1943. The Mt. Clare shops, which stretched from Poppleton to Carey streets, along Pratt Street, employed thousands of workers throughout the 19th and 20th centuries.

Chapter 3: WEST

107. Davidge Hall, University of Maryland School of Medicine's oldest building, was bedecked for a celebration in 1907. The 1812 building, with its circular anatomical theater, stands at Lombard and Greene streets. It was designed by Robert Cary Long.

108. Broadcasting the gospel by motorbus is the Rev. G.E. Lowman. His pulpit was a collapsible platform on the rear of his omnibus. The loudspeaker amplified his voice, March 22, 1930, at 721 W. Hamburg Street.

109. All of Baltimore's public parks once had their own resident groundskeepers and police. This gentleman was in charge of Carroll Park in August, 1909. Carroll Park was created on the 18th century estate of Charles Carroll, the Barrister.

110. Ceremonies marking the beginning of a restoration for the Babe Ruth birth place, 216 Emory Street, were held July 8, 1969, in the Ridgely's Delight neighborhood. The house is now a public museum.

111. The corner of Washington Boulevard and Fremont Avenue appeared this way March 26, 1932. In the distance is the Bromo Seltzer bottle, atop the Emerson Drug Company's headquarters. The camera is looking east, along Washington Boulevard. ''From about age 13 to the time I went off to World War II at 18, we lived on Washington Boulevard. Circumstances were poor, to say the least. My father

had a dry goods store then. We lived above it. There was no heat in any of the rooms . . . In those days of the middle and late 1930s, there was a Pratt branch library on a side street around the corner from my father's store . . . When I wasn't at the main library, I was there,'' recollected Jerome M. Edelstein, National Gallery of Art chief librarian.

112. In 1943, the Pratt began bookwagon service to bring books to some of the city's poor neighborhoods where residents had not learned to use a branch library. The horse and wagon were rented for $2 a day from a local stable. Margaret A. Edwards, who conceived and ran the service, later wrote, "It was a handsome, hawkers' red vegetable wagon, low slung, with yellow shafts and wheels." The wagon's arrival was announced by a "xylophone with four notes, which served the purpose admirably but became unbearable if played too long and too near by strong-muscled and enthusiastic young patrons. . . . from the first day there was never any doubt of the suc-

cess of the project. . . . the boys of the neighborhood were only too ready to help with Betty (the horse) and soon the position of horse-boy was open only to those who deserved special consideration for helpfulness or who had improved in behavior so much they deserved a reward. Because Baltimore people are accustomed to sitting on their famous white steps on summer evenings and because more volunteer help was available in the afternoons and evenings, the book wagon operated from four o'clock in the afternoon until it became too dark to distinguish one title from another.''

113. On June 20, 1942, these Southwest Baltimore children posed as the local unit of the Junior Victory Army stationed in the 200 block of South Vincent Street, between Pratt and McHenry streets.

114. A group congregated around the Westport Bank, 2219 Annapolis Road, February, 1940.

115. Opposite, Montgomery Ward's Washington Boulevard and Monroe Street retail store was packed with customers for a 1958 Washington's Birthday sale.

116. When the Hollins Market celebrated its centennial in September 1936, more than 15,000 persons watched a gala parade through West Baltimore. Christian J. Eitemiller, whose large Arlington Avenue and Hollins Street grocery store faced the market, organized the centennial. The market once spilled several blocks eastward as merchants set up outdoor stalls in the bed of Hollins Street on the market days of Thursday, Friday and Saturday. Prices were higher near or in the market shed; bargains were sold in the open-air block, between Arlington Avenue and Schroeder Street. Writer William Stump said in 1957: "Veteran shoppers start their tour leisurely, buying their meat from one of the butchers who came to the market as apprentice boys at about the time Dewey steamed into Manila Bay."

117. Westport Pratt Library, No. 27, opened January 22, 1929 at Annapolis Road and Indiana Street. For nearly five years the neighborhood campaigned for the new branch. It would have opened sooner had not the basement filled with water and the heating plant broken. Louise Webster, 410 Maryland Avenue, Westport, was the first child to borrow a book. Much in demand that first day were copies of "Hans Brinker" and "King Arthur."

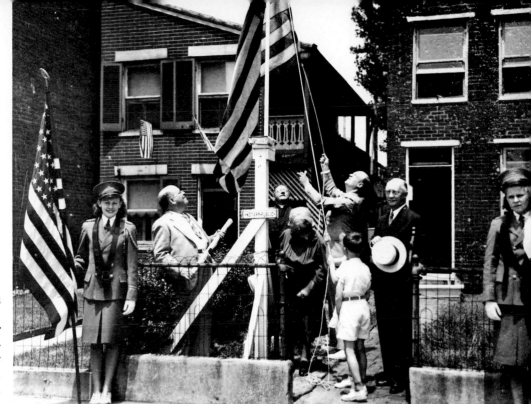

118. On June 14, 1940, the local patriots unfurled the colors at 1206 Hollins Street. In the group behind the fence are Arthur Buxbaum, Rev. Fr. Placidus Rattenberger, O.S.B., pastor of Fourteen Holy Martyrs Church, Mrs. Buxbaum, Capt. Richard O'Connell and William Norris. The others are unidentified.

119. A gas lamp and a misspelled street sign attract attention at Hollins and Callender streets, March 19, 1930. This old Irish and German neighborhood was once home to Baltimore and Ohio Railroad workers.

121. The Sisters of the Congregation of the Good Shepherd ran a home for wayward girls at Mount and Hollins streets, from 1864 to 1965. This 1910 photograph shows the sisters in their choir, which was separated from their chapel altar by a cloister screen. The complex of buildings included Willow Brook, a fine 1799 residence, which was donated to the sisters by Emily Caton McTavish, granddaughter of Charles Carroll of Carrollton. When Willow Brook was demolished in 1966, an oval-shaped room was dismantled and reinstalled in the Baltimore Museum of Art.

122. The Cummings florist shop, 1123 West Baltimore Street, was neatly outfitted with a white-tiled floor and wicker furnishings in the late 1920s.

120. Opposite, dignified and quiet old Waverly Terrace, the 100 block of North Carcy Street, faced Franklin Square. This atmospheric photo was taken on August 29, 1909. Though the street was lined with bushy trees, many of the homes had striped canvas awnings to cut down the hot, setting afternoon sun. Several of the second-floor balconies were covered with vines. The block was constructed about 1850 as private residences.

123. Women operate sewing machines to make pajamas at the Krestle Manufacturing Company, Pulaski and McHenry streets, about

1937. Garment manufacturing was once one of Baltimore's major industries and a large employer of women.

124. Children of St. Martin's Catholic Church, Fayette Street and Fulton Avenue, march in a May procession, May 22, 1932. The annual procession was a major event in West Baltimore when the congregation numbered 9,000. The church was founded in 1865.

125. A hot 1920s night on the Calhoun Street side of Franklin Square drew a crowd to the park. Franklin Square lent its name to a hospital that faced the square. Student nurses were required to take an hour's walk before bedtime in the park's gardens.

126. Children line up to withdraw books from the Pratt's Branch 2, Hollins and Calhoun streets, April, 1947. Writer Russell Baker, who grew up around the corner on Lombard Street, discovered the library in the 1930s. He described it as a "whimsical little cathedral, as it were, to the printed word." H.L. Mencken also used this branch, which was one of the original four planned by Enoch Pratt. The library operation was moved to a new building at Hollins and Payson streets in 1964.

127. Patients rested in Franklin Square Hospital's sun parlor, Calhoun and Fayette Streets, about 1910. "Doctors did not bring a patient in unless something was very wrong. Practically every appendix was ruptured and half the pneumonia cases were fatal. . . . We often worked around the clock in wards jammed with typhoid cases," wrote nurse Myrtle G. Morris of her student days there. The hospital moved to Baltimore County in 1969.

128. The American Stores, later known as the Acme, had a grocery operation at Frederick and Millington avenues, April 11, 1932. Just across the street was a tourist home. Many West Baltimore beef and pork butchers lived in this neighborhood.

129. A streetcar rider awaits a car on a rainy day at Edmondson Avenue and Schroeder Street in the middle 1920s.

130. The beer flowed at Paul Hoffman's saloon, Mosher and Vincent streets, about 1906. In that year Baltimore had about 20 different brands of beer, including the products of the Wiessner, Gottlieb, Bauernschmidt & Straus, Moerlein, Duke-hart and Gunther breweries.

131. The ground known as Lafayette Square, Lafayette, Carrollton and Arlington avenues and Lanvale Street, was purchased by the city for $15,000 in 1857. It was used as a Union soldiers' camping ground during the Civil War. In 1873 the square got its own bronze fountain. "Beds of various designs, cultivated in cannas and coleus, some containing as many as 13 varieties of foliage and flowering plants, attest the skill with which the square is kept," wrote Baltimore historian J. Thomas Scharf in 1881. The 1100 block of West Lafayette Avenue overlooks Lafayette Square in this March 1937 photo.

132. When John "Frank" Kelly died February 9, 1928, he was considered the most influential Democrat in Baltimore. He was also known as "The Kelly," and lived modestly at 1106 West Saratoga Street. Hundreds attended his funeral, shown here. His throne room was the basement. "A path was worn down the cellar stairs by beggars and political suppliants, by governors, senators and some of the mayors eager for his nod for a future candidacy. Every morning Kelly walked to Lexington Market, doling out money to outstretched hands or promising to put coal in the cellar of an unfortunate family. His Christmas gift baskets were numerous," wrote Ralph J. Sybert of Kelly's style.

133. A Number 8 streetcar is headed into town at congested Frederick and Caton avenues in 1948. This busy corner was a major traffic sticking point. The Pennsylvania Railroad's mainline to Washington crossed under Frederick Avenue at this point.

134. Workers repair a street at Frederick and Fonthill avenues in August 1927 as a Number 8 streetcar heads for Catonsville.

135. In October 1943, School 68, the Betsy Ross School, Millington Avenue and Lehman Street, put on a patriotic pageant occasioned by World War II.

136. Crowd at the dedication of St. Joseph's Monastery Church, October 2, 1932, Monastery Avenue and Old Frederick Road, Irvington. The Passionist fathers established a monastery here in 1867-68. It was then in the far western suburbs of Baltimore.

137. Opposite, a student tries to master a Linotype machine at St. Mary's Industrial School, April 4, 1924. Printing was one of the several trades taught there. Some years earlier Babe Ruth was enrolled here and taught how to play baseball. The buildings now house Cardinal Gibbons High School.

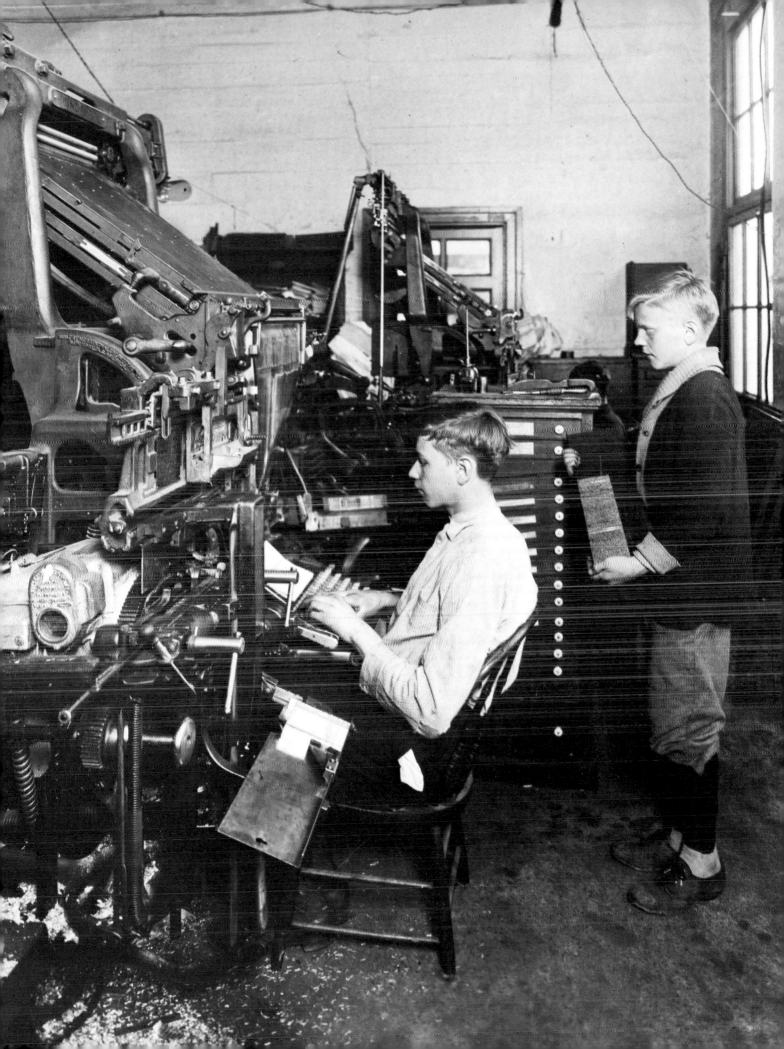

138. The intersection of Poplar Grove and Franklin streets in September, 1950. These mothers are walking their children to school. Edmondson Avenue is in the background, which also includes an Arundel ice cream store branch and Ludwig's drug store.

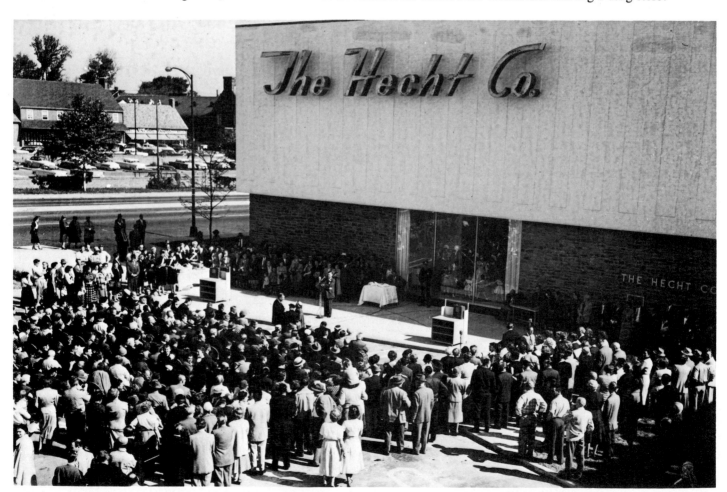

139. The Hecht Company's Edmondson Village store was dedicated October 15, 1956. The former department store is now the Westside Skills Center. Across the street is the Edmondson Village Shopping Center, a colonial-style group of shops which opened in 1947. The Pratt's Edmondson Avenue Library, Branch No. 28, is to the east. The library was dedicated July 31, 1952. Library service began here December 1943 in a Charing Cross Road building donated by the Welsh Construction Company. The library was later given free space by the developer of the Edmondson Village shopping center until a permanent Pratt branch was constructed.

140. The annual visit of the circus brought the big top to West Baltimore and a vacant lot at Edmondson Avenue and Bentalou Street. Here the balloon man finds two willing customers.

141. It seemed that every Baltimore residential block had its corner store. It sold everything from canned goods to newspapers, snow balls to shoe laces. This version was at Lafayette Avenue and Monroe streets, February 28, 1938.

142. Opposite, workmen are covering a stream branch that ran through Walbrook about 1908. The view looks north on the 1700 and 1800 blocks of Poplar Grove Street, just south of North Avenue.

143. Coppery barked sycamore trees surround Pratt's Branch 17, Easterwood Park, North Avenue near Smallwood Street, in the 1930s. The branch opened in June 1914 and closed in January, 1953, when a new North Avenue branch opened. The library was designed with a distinctive Middle Eastern flair.

144. These West Baltimore bicyclists are off to Catonsville September 12, 1893.

145. A group of well dressed Baltimoreans dropped a fishing pole in the Gwynns Falls millrace in the summer of 1899. The water from this stream once powered several mills. As the city acquired this area as a public park, the millrace would be filled in and made into a walking path. The purchase of Gwynns Falls and Leakin parks was advocated by the Olmsted Brothers, the visionary landscape architects who advised the city on public improvements. They wanted the city to preserve its natural stream valleys from development.

146. Baltimore's Inner Harbor was a working waterfront in the late 1930s. The camera looks south on Light Street. The McCormick spice plant is the most prominent of Light Street buildings. Nearby were the Globe brewery, Maryland Biscuit, American Tobacco and Heywood Brothers Chair Manufacturing companies. The American Ice plant is on Key Highway at the foot of Federal Hill.

Chapter 4: SOUTH

147. Watermelon boats docked along Pratt Street, August 21, 1897.

148. The male office staff of the Baltimore Steam Packet Company, better known as the Old Bay Line, about 1915, was quartered in an office on Light, near Barre streets. The building had a wooden clock tower. Chesapeake Bay steamers made the 185-mile run to Norfolk.

149. Baltimore's busiest thoroughfare was Light Street, shown here after widening in April, 1913. The view is looking north from Barre Street, near what today would be the Light Street Pavilion of Harborplace.

150. St. Mary's Star of the Sea Catholic Church, Riverside Avenue and Gittings Street, had a gas light placed inside a cross atop its Gothic steeple. The light guided mariners up the Baltimore harbor. Later electrified, the light with its lens is shown here during some repair work in the late 1920s. The church, which once had a large Irish congregation, was built in 1869.

152. Compton Street, between Hamburg and Cross streets, was one of South Baltimore's tiny thoroughfares. The Gothic steeple is that of Holy Cross Catholic Church on West Street. Compton Street's houses have been nearly all demolished.

153. A watermelon wagon calls at homes in the 100 block of East Montgomery Street in the 1930s.

151. Opposite, three South Baltimoreans pass an old wood fence and garden at Sanders Street and Riverside Avenue in July, 1940. Years later, film director Alfred Hitchcock used Sanders Street for a shot in his ''Marnie.''

154. Casino Theatre, at 1118 Light Street, got a stylish new marquee in the late 1930s. "Mystery Man," with Bud Armstrong, was the feature. Down the street are C. D. Rudolph's hardware, an F. W. Woolworth dime store and Silverman's clothing shop.

155. Southern High School students congregate outside Peter's Confectionery, Warren Avenue and William Street, in October 1954.

156. Southern Police station was a landmark at Patapsco and Ostend streets since it was built in 1896. Here a group of South Baltimore children cluster around the lockup in 1935. Writer Spencer Davidson said in 1955, "The best compliment to the Southern station house is to describe it as a building where 400 youngsters come and go unafraid. About 400 of them are enrolled in a boy's club operating on the second floor. In the course of a summer day it seems 4,000 must use the water cooler near the side entrance."

157. The Casino Theatre, 1118 Light Street, was known earlier as the Majestic and the Brodie, named after a South Baltimore clothing store owner. Next to the movie house are the George Karangelen lunch room, Israel Miller's clothing, and an A&P.

158. In the days of 15-cents-a-gallon gasoline, W. L. Breeding ran a Spanish-style Sinclair filling station at Key Highway and Jackson street. The clock says "Sherwood service," indicating the station belonged to John Sherwood, who created Sherwood Gardens in Guilford.

159. Coney Island hot dogs, locally made by the Goetze firm, were featured in the 1400 block of Light Street, at Fort Avenue, in the 1920s. The Garden confectionery store is just across Light Street.

160. A shopper passes the Cross Street Market, Light and Cross streets, in October, 1952. Signs indicate a Fidelity Trust branch, an Arundel ice cream store and the McHenry movie theater on the left, with a Rice's bakery, the Four Besche Brothers furniture store and Morstein's jewelers on the right. In the distance are the Maryland National Bank building and McCormick's advertising symbol of a vanilla bottle atop its Light Street spice plant.

161. F.S. and G.L. Brown workers pose at the machine and engineering plant, 20-26 East Fort Avenue, 1897.

162. A Pratt Library branch came to Locust Point in October 1910. In 1928 it moved to School 76, the Francis Scott Key School, and was dedicated to the memory of Persis K. Miller, the school's principal. The branch closed in June 1957, about ten years after this photo.

163. An October 27, 1917 cyclone swept through Locust Point and did considerable damage to Fort Avenue and Latrobe Park Terrace homes. **The Baltimore American** reported, ''Wild excitement prevailed for several hours, children ran screeching through the streets . . .'' The storm pulled walls from houses and exposed interior rooms. But, in the case of this heavily damaged barber shop, glass vases were left undisturbed and resting on a mantel.

164. Members of the Maryland Swimming Club, whose clubhouse was on the site of the Dundalk Marine Terminal, take to the Patapsco's Middle Branch near the Hanover Street Bridge in the 1920s. The club was founded in 1903 and for the next 25 years turned

out some of the state's best athletes. The club sponsored sailing, canoeing, tennis, baseball, soccer and track, in addition to swimming.

165. The busy corner of Hanover Street and Patapsco Avenue got new traffic signals and pedestrian walk lights October 23, 1953.

166. Gypsies camped at Cherry Hill, August 18, 1921. The city chased them out of town with charges of health violations.

167. Opposite, a hot July, 1942 day at the Bethlehem Fairfield shipyard. During World War II the yards employed 47,000 persons on around-the-clock shifts. The famous Liberty and Victory ships were launched here.

168. Baltimore's dock workers went on strike in May 1922. There were localized riots. This photo, taken May 3, 1922, on Thames Street just east of Broadway, shows a group of workers who earlier in the day had boarded the ship Newark and forced 20 of its crew members off. The strike protested a wage cut.

Chapter 5: **EAST**

169. Typical of many Baltimore neighborhood grocery stores was that owned by Vincent Garofolo at 1007 East Lombard Street in Baltimore's Italian neighborhood, 1926.

170. Vincent Garofolo's grocery store offered local brands — Rice's and Koester's bread and Lord Calvert coffee, ground on the spot. Early each morning the bakeries dropped off loaves of bread baked overnight. Shelves were lined with lithograph-labeled cans. The grocery was one of several in Baltimore's Little Italy community. Throughout the years, the neighborhood has retained its ethnic traditions. Local tradition holds that Italians who sailed from Italy in the 19th Century settled in East Baltimore because of its proximity to the President Street station.

171. Opposite, St. Leo's School drum and bugle corps signed up to join the Junior Victory Army, June 21, 1942, to help fight World War II on the home front.

173. This was the city's first public bath house, built by philanthropist Henry Walters. It opened in May 1900 at 131 South High Street. At its dedication, Walters said he hoped the bath would be run "on the good old democratic principle of the greatest good to the greatest number." The bath houses offered public bathing and laundry rooms when bathtubs and indoor plumbing were scarce in Baltimore's poor neighborhoods. The public baths were out of business by the 1950s.

174. The strictly disciplined charges of the German General Orphan Asylum work in the laundry, 224 Aisquith Street, in 1915. The girls were trained for domestic service. The imposing red-brick building held about 150 boys and girls and left the old neighborhood for Catonsville in the 1920s. "We wore identical clothes, marched in procession through the streets when we went to school and to church, and we filed in procession to meals and went to bed under the watchful eyes of the superintendent or his assistant," wrote Ernest Johannesen of his boyhood years there.

172. Opposite, the Folly Theatre, destroyed by fire on March 28, 1928, is shown here about seven years earlier. It was at 727-729 East Baltimore Street and was built as the Monumental. It later became a burlesque house and served as a Yiddish theater. A 1920 newspaper ad promoted a burlesque show with "30 dainty widows on the electric runway." John McGrath described the old playhouse: "The people downstairs were noisy and demonstrative, but it was the gallery gods that put zest into their stamping feet, applauding and hissing. . . . Everybody bought newspapers . . . and threw them at unpopular actors."

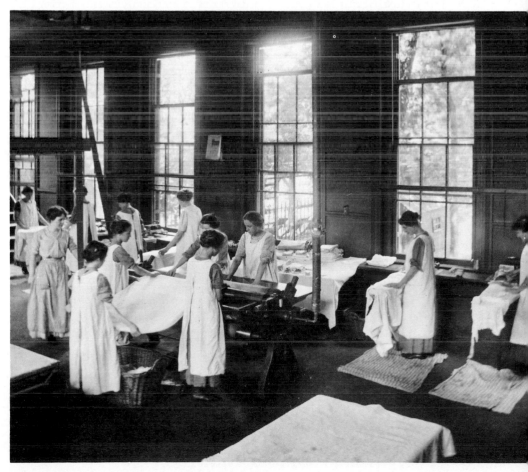

175. This middle 1930s view looks south on the west side of Exeter Street from Watson Street and shows an elaborate iron balcony on the corner house. Jewish merchants tended small shops that sold everything from tea to clothespins.

176. The curbside Lombard Street Market stretched from Exeter Street to Central Avenue. As it was a Middle European Jewish neighborhood, the merchants sold Middle European Jewish foods. The fish dealer sold carp in a white-tiled pool in his shop's front window. Chickens, ducks and geese were also live and piled high in wooden cages on the street. The photo is from the late 1920s.

177. "The narrow sidewalks, further constricted by an overflow of merchandise from abutting shops, are jammed with stout housewives, baby carriages, barrels of pickled fish, pyramids of fruit, bolts of fabric, chicken coops, mounds of tinware, crates of china and what-have-you," noted **The Evening Sun** on Sept. 22, 1939.

178. The first block of South High Street was noisy and busy on Sept. 14, 1934. The view looks toward Watson Street. On the right is the Coney Island bath house. The block was lined with rooming houses, homes and small shops.

179. Baltimore's Jewish community established a number of charitable institutions, including the Hebrew Home for Incurables on Aisquith Street. Some of its oldest residents were photographed here about 1912.

180. A streetcar split a switch at Baltimore and Aisquith streets on July 13, 1943, jumped the tracks and rammed a pole. Streetcar accidents created a neighborhood event for curious onlookers. Many of the passengers would be examined by a physician, and several

would no doubt wind up in litigation with the Baltimore Transit Company. The McKim Free School building is in the background.

181. The Pratt's Branch 11, 6 South Central Avenue, was crowded in November 1932. The branch was originally organized by The Maccabeans, a Jewish philanthropic organization that financially underwrote a small library station. The store-front operation began December 14, 1904, with Marie Bloch as the librarian. She spoke and wrote English, Russian, German, Yiddish and Hebrew and was helpful to immigrants who had just encountered English. The station became one of the largest circulation points in the whole system and graduated to its own branch building in 1921.

182. During a severe cold snap in the winter of 1921, Mayor William F. Broening ordered the distribution of free wood to the needy. Here the city's chief executive tours conditions in a poor Central Avenue neighborhood.

183. An East Baltimore street scene — the 900 block of Aisquith Street — was photographed in the summer of 1939. The typical Baltimore block, with its corner store, faced the Institute of Notre Dame.

184. Librarian Bonnie D. Peasant Lee spins a children's hour tale in Pratt Library Branch 5, 816 North Broadway at Miller Street, in the late 1940s. The branch opened in 1888 and closed in 1971 when a new Broadway branch opened.

185. Students at the Paul L. Dunbar Junior-Senior High School, Caroline and McElderry streets, assemble airplane models during the World War II years. Before Baltimore' schools were desegregated, Dunbar was one of the larger black secondary schools.

186. The 1000 block of East Fayette Street, between Colvin and Exeter, was photographed in October 1936 before its demolition for slum clearance. These buildings were razed in 1936-37 to widen Fayette Street. Units of public housing would follow.

188. Broadway was one of the grand streets of East Baltimore. Its center boulevard strip was planted with grass and flower beds, laid with walks, fountains and benches. The Johns Hopkins Hospital is in the distance in this 1915 view, south from North Avenue.

189. The automobile made an impact on Baltimore in the 1920s. This early car rental agency was in the 800 block of Greenmount Avenue in 1927.

187. Opposite, flags fly from the 1000 block of Broadway on May 10, 1911, for Broadway Visiting Day, an East Baltimore parade and carnival. The best-decorated house got $10. This block contained the losers. One sidewalk is smooth-paved, while its neighbor has the old brick paving. In 1927, H.L. Mencken lamented the brick sidewalks' passing. He said there was an ''insane war against the noble old brick sidewalks of Baltimore, seeking to replace them with slippery and glaring concrete.''

190. The Hasslinger family was known for its prepared seafood sold in Baltimore neighborhoods. This 1406 Harford Avenue operation dated from 1932, when a dollar would have bought enough crab cakes for a party.

191. The sun reflects off these Formstone-covered homes in the 2000 block Portugal Street as residents make the best a hot July 1967 day.

192. The S.B. Pollard delivery wagon makes its rounds at Ashland Avenue and Chester Street about 1913. Many old Baltimore neighborhoods still have back alley stables that quartered the horses used for general service throughout the city.

193. The 1963 summer heat drove the children of East Madison Street's Latrobe Homes to this recreational sprinkler system maintained by the city.

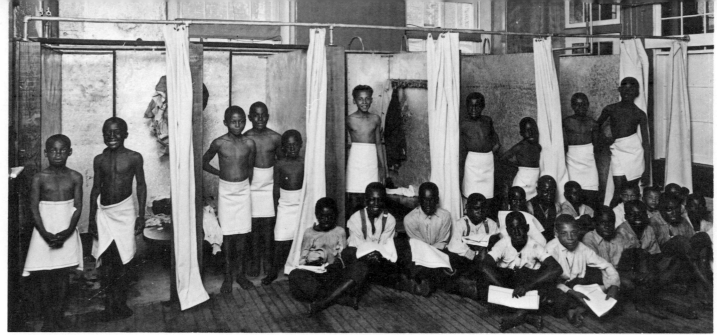

194. The city maintained an extensive public bath system and would use schools or other public buildings when housing in poor neighborhoods lacked indoor plumbing. This 1922 bath scene is at School 108, Caroline near Bank streets.

195. Neighborhood markets once served a local clientele. Simpson's meat markets, which had four East Baltimore shops, delivered to customers via horse and wagon about 1915.

196. The Northeast Market at Monument, Chester and Duncan streets still served German and Bohemian neighborhoods when this 1946 photograph was taken. The old market building was completed in 1885. A market favorite was mead, a cooling drink made from yeast and spices.

197. In the early 1950s, East Baltimore's neighborhood streets were still lined with thriving shops, businesses that were often 50 or 60 years old. William Engelhardt's hardware store was a classic of its kind at Oliver, Gay and Washington streets.

198. The torso murder case was one of the city's most celebrated crimes. Newspapers played up the lurid events surrounding the death of Evelyn Rice, who lived in the tiny 100 block of South Durham Street. Parts of her body were found in East Baltimore sewer drains in April 1939. Here the coroner removed the head, which had been buried in the garden behind her home. An East Baltimore steelworker was charged, convicted and sent to prison.

199. The steeple of St. Patrick's Catholic Church is visible on the left, with the Broadway Market house in the center of the 1880s stereo-card view of Broadway, south from Baltimore Street. Broadway was then a wide, important East Baltimore street. Only a small portion of it was paved.

200. Sr. Mary Maurice tried her black Oxfords at hopscotch in the St. Patrick's School yard in 1959. Sisters Diona, Joanella and Germanus watch the scene from the porch.

201. The intersection of Broadway and Eastern Avenue saw plenty of traffic in 1936. The new Chevrolets were just off the Broening Highway assembly line.

202. In February 1905, Highlandtown had its own pasta factory, the Maryland Macaroni Works in the 4200 block of East Baltimore Street. An ad for the firm said, "Made in the best equipped factory in the world, of finest spring wheat flour, by Italian natives who know how, and under the most approved and sanitary conditions."

203. Librarian Sara L. Siebert and patrons at the Pratt Library's Fells Point Branch 19, 606 South Ann Street. She wrote about this neighborhood in 1957, "On a foggy night when river sounds and smells reach the northern border of the eastside and the remaining gaslights throw a pale yellow glow through the murk; when a thin-faced urchin drags a can of home fuel over the stone blocks of Aliceanna Street; when a blue-jeaned seaman weaves some fancy steps before disappearing around the curve of the Thames Street crescent, the London and Dickensian atmosphere is very close and real."

205. The back door to an East Baltimore rowhouse provides the background for this family snapshot scene.

206. George Kerr stands at attention in his Sunday-best suit in the backyard of 7 North Kenwood Avenue in 1918.

204. Opposite, Prohibition put an end to merry scenes such as this, the Franz B. Amend tavern, 3400 Eastern Avenue, Highlandtown, about 1915. With so many German families in Baltimore, brewing was a major industry here.

207. Polish families settled Fells Point in the 1890s. Local tradition contends that they crossed the Atlantic on North German Lloyd steamers, got off at Locust Point, then took the municipally operated ferry across the Patapsco to Fells Point, where they made their homes and established themselves. The Sadowski funeral home was at 703 South Ann Street.

208. The tug Ada visited the Canton waterfront about 1910. Canton was named for Canton, China, but the Southeast Baltimore waterfront neighborhood became home to Welsh, German, Irish and Polish immigrants.

209. Opening day for a Patterson Park children's wading pool in June 1938 was as much an event as the closing of school. The park's first swimming pool opened in August 1906 and has seen heavy use during Baltimore's hot summers. The park has been called East Baltimore's front yard and back yard. During the Civil War, the park served as a Union hospital camp.

210. The Tin Decorating Company of Baltimore, Boston Street and Linwood Avenue, was established in 1914. Workers produced decorated tin candy and cake boxes, baskets, mugs and plates. The American Tobacco Company's green Lucky Strike tin cigarette boxes were once stamped here. Examples of "Tindeco" products are today sought by collectors.

211. Local committees established strategic points to boost Second World War bond sales. Eastern Avenue and Conkling Street, the commercial heart of Highlandtown, was a natural choice in July 1942. Local orchestras, politicians and personalities all got in the act.

212. Baltimore jazz specialist and restaurant owner Harley Brinsfield gives an informal lesson in jazz history at the Pratt's Patterson Park Branch No. 13, Linwood Avenue and Fayette Street, May 16, 1956. The student wears a Patterson Park High School sweater. Harley's jazz program was once broadcast nightly on Baltimore radio stations.

213. The return of nylon stockings after World War II was a major retailing event. Irvin's, at 3428 Eastern Avenue, had customers waiting in line for the real thing in 1946.

214. Haussner's restaurant, "famous for fine food and fine art," was established in 1926 by William H. Haussner at 3313 Eastern Avenue. Its collection of 19th-century French and German academic paintings was not as well recognized in 1951, this photo's date, as it is today.

215. East Baltimoreans form a line for the sugar-ration coupons at the William Paca School No. 83, Lakewood Avenue and Fayette

216. In 1947, a Red Rocket No. 26 streetcar pair takes the dip under the Highlandtown Pennsylvania Railroad overpass at Eastern Avenue. The cars, which once shuttled thousands of East Baltimore workers, have just left the Highlandtown shopping district.

Street, on a hot July morning in 1942.

217. Post-war brought a demand for autos. Assembly line workers at the Broening Highway Chevrolet Plant put the finishing touches on 1946 models. The plant is one of the city's major employers.

218. Logan Field was once the aviation pride of the city. The early flying field was named for Lt. Patrick Henry Logan, a young Army flyer and stunt pilot who crashed here and died July 5, 1920. During the aviation-crazy 1920s several large air meets were held here, such as this September 1922 aeronautic convention involving the Army, Navy, Marines and Maryland National Guard, as well as

American, French, German and British aircraft. More than 1,000 spectators watched two Marine aviators crash and die when their engines failed. The city and state eventually helped underwrite Logan Field's expenses. Flying greats Amelia Earhart and Charles Lindbergh visited the field, which lasted through World War II but was then plowed up for veterans' housing as Logan Village.

219. The 5600 block of Harford Road was considerably less busy April 13, 1929, when most people traveled by streetcar. The view looks south toward Hamilton Avenue. The Hamilton Presbyterian Church is on the right, at Evergreen Avenue. After World War II, this area would experience rapid growth as housing developments, highways and shopping centers altered the face of Northeast Baltimore.

Chapter 6: **NORTHEAST**

220. Sears, Roebuck and Company's North Avenue and Harford Road store was one of the city's main selling operations in the late 1940s. The big store opened with great flourish September 21, 1938. The event was carried live on local radio. The modernistic store, designed by Chicago architects Nimmons, Carr and Wright, closed in 1981.

221. Hillen Road's Mergenthaler Vocational Technical High School offered a baking course. These students enjoys a day's work: Barbara German, Dennis Stielper and Peter Mooney, on the steps, and, left to right on rail, Rae Wilson, David Quoos and Nancy Barnes, May 20, 1958.

222. Led by Dean Albert N. Whiting and Dr. Martin P. Jenkins, president of Morgan State College, students and faculty process in a convocation, September 1962.

223. These Elkader Road homes, built by the E.J. Gallagher Realty Company, were offered for sale in the fall of 1931. Ednor Gardens was named for Edward and Norman Gallagher, the firm founder's two sons. By this time, the Baltimore rowhouse facade was taking on new designs such as this Elizabethan model. It sold for about $4,000. Ednor Gardens is due north of Memorial Stadium.

224. The employees of the Cohen, Goldman Clothing Manufacturing gather outside their shop in the 2200 block of Aisquith Street, May 2, 1947, following a daring $24,602 payroll robbery. Six masked bandits, armed with pistols and other weapons, entered the building after the payroll had been delivered by armored car. Workers shouted for help from windows, but passersby thought it was a joke. The crime was never solved.

225. In 1929, the Roland Park Company purchased 530 acres of wooded land in Northeast Baltimore and named the proposed development Northwood. The first homes were begun in September 1930. Because of economic conditions during the Depression, only 87 homes were constructed up to 1937. Many were designed by architect John A. Ahlers, who also laid out the curving streets. At that time a lot was $1,825 and a house could be constructed for $8,500. This is a Roundtop Road scene in December 1957, when the neighborhood was largely complete. Today the neighborhood calls itself Original Northwood.

226. After a lengthy supermarket workers' strike, customers made up for lost time at the Alameda Shopping Center, 5600 The Alameda, in June 1964.

227. Northwood got its own 30,000 book Pratt Library branch, Branch 10, on April 20, 1960. The ground at 4420 Loch Raven Boulevard was donated by Mr. and Mrs. Milton Schwaber, who built a shopping center near the library site.

228. Students and teachers at Leith Walk Elementary School, Leith Walk and Sherwood Avenue, held a balloon ascension on May 15, 1963.

229. Integration of places of public accommodation was controversial in the early 1960s. Mrs. Ruth Lighston buys tickets to enter the Northwood Theater, Havenwood Road off Loch Raven Boulevard, on February 22, 1963. She and her children were the first blacks to enter the previously segregated movie house.

139

230. The Clifton Park swimming pool, seen here on June 14, 1921, was a Northeast Baltimore institution, where thousands of children learned to swim. Opening day of public swimming was as closely watched as the day public school closed. The city charged three cents an hour to swim at public pools. That price got you a bathing suit, towel and use of one of the pool's 350 lockers. In the background is Baltimore and Ohio Railroad main line to Philadelphia.

231. Clifton Park began as a gentleman's country seat. The park belonged to merchant-philanthropist Johns Hopkins, who maintained its 250 acres with flower gardens, walks and groves as a summer estate. He planned that after his death it be used for his university. This never happened. The city purchased Clifton in 1895 and soon enlarged it with additional acreage. The park's old gardens, walks and greenhouses were maintained. This 1912 group of Lauraville residents was photographed on a rustic bridge on park grounds. By 1950, the public use of Clifton's tennis courts, swimming pool, band shell, golf course and baseball diamonds was the heaviest in the city.

232. Weber's Park, along Harford Road near Lauraville, was a gathering spot in the 1890s and early years of the 20th century.

233. The Clifton Park golf course was the first public course in the city. It opened in May 1916 when the game was so new the city dared not charge a greens fee for the use of the course. The game soon caught on and the Clifton links were nearly always filled with scenes resembling this 1920s shot.

234. The No. 22 bus served a busy crosstown route. Here passengers board a vehicle headed for Highlandtown at Harford Road and 32nd Street on July 1, 1952.

235. Chesapeake and Potomac Telephone Company workers lay Western Electric cables along the 5200 block of Harford Road near Echodale Avenue in the late 1920s. The houses in the background are now demolished. The old Hamilton telephone exchange was established in August 1906 and served 69 subscribers.

237. Opposite, Bishop Thomas J. Toolen of Mobile laid the cornerstone of St. Francis of Assisi Church, Harford Road and Chesterfield Avenue, on May 15, 1927. The open fields in the background are part of Herring Run Park. A new church was begun on the site in 1952 and completed two years later.

236. Panorama of Montebello Park on March 30, 1913. Over the years the vacant lots would fill up with new cottages. The photo was taken in the vicinity of Grindon Avenue, off Harford Road. Cottages sold for about $1,500.

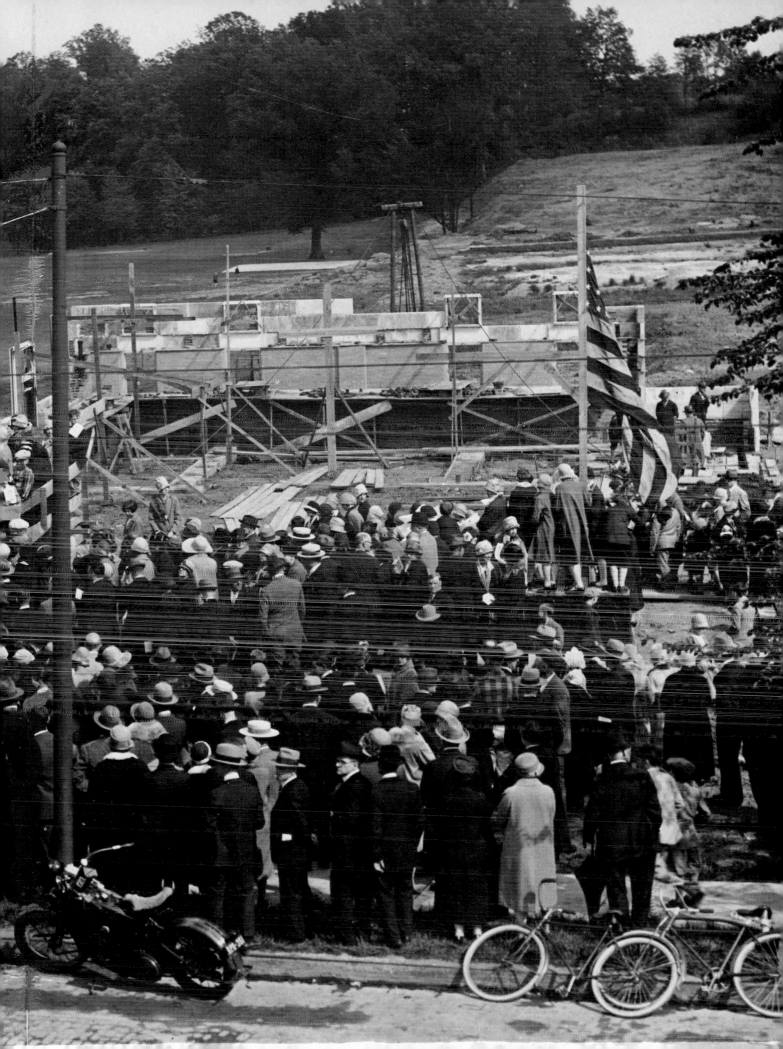

238. The family of Mrs. John S. League stands outside 4306 Arabia Avenue in June 1932. Many of Northeast Baltimore's residential streets are lined with bungalows and solid, well-maintained middle-class homes such as this.

239. These Ailsa Avenue residents in Lauraville decorated their frame home in patriotic finery during the summer of 1911. Lauraville was still regarded as distant country to most Baltimoreans who then lived in rowhouse neighborhoods closer to the center of the city.

240. A 1912 parade gathers outside the Lauraville House restaurant and tavern, 4536 Harford Road. For more than 50 years the restaurant was operated by John C. Munders — father and son — who established this popular gathering place the year this photo was taken. John Munder Jr. was well known in Northeast Baltimore as a local politician and sporting figure. Munder's rathskeller was reported to have been the best in Northeast Baltimore.

241. A 1910 outing with the Hamilton volunteer fire company included an open-air omnibus. The fire brigade used outings and carnivals to purchase fire-fighting equipment.

242. The Hamilton volunteer fire company was one of the community's main gathering spots on Hamilton Avenue. The company had a system of ringing a large bell that told the members the approximate location of a fire. In 1910, the community was in Baltimore County.

243. The annual May procession at St. Dominic's Catholic Church in Hamilton was a major neighborhood event. The parish was composed largely of Irish and Italian families in May 1939 when the procession advanced along Harford Road.

244. The business heart of Hamilton was the corner of Harford Road and Hamilton Avenue, shown here in March 1930. The No. 19 streetcar was the neighborhood's main transportation link, but automobiles were clearly on the ascendancy. Purdum's drug store, Tames general store and the Arcade theater were Hamilton business landmarks.

245. Harford Road was making the transition from country road to city street when this October 1927 shot was taken at Gibbons Avenue. The view looks north.

246. The west side of the 5400 block of Harford Road, Hamilton, included these businesses in March of 1930: Joseph Moreland's real estate office, Riehl's bakery, an American grocery store, Harrison's pharmacy, Israel Schleider's Harford department store and a lunchroom.

247. The Hamilton Little Leaguers parade down Harford Road at Northern Parkway, May 14, 1956.

248. The 1928 view shows Belair Road, looking south across Herring Run Park. The city had just repaved the old turnpike, which was then developing as a major thoroughfare. Trolley cars on the No. 15 line operated in the middle of the street until 1963.

249. In the 1930s the Herring Run Park area clung to its rural origins. Here a group of recreational horseback riders cross the old Brehms Lane Bridge over Herring Run. Brehms Lane was named after George Brehm, a Bavarian brewer whose slogan was "One Grade Only." Baltimore beer drinkers asked for his light lager by calling for "O.G.O."

250. The girls' Catholic High School opened in September 1939 at Edison Highway and Elmley Avenue. The school was planned to serve the populations that were then moving out of old city neighborhoods into the semi-suburban bungalows of Northeast Baltimore. The building was designed by Washington architect Frederick Vernon Murphy.

252. Wicker chairs, concrete urns and snake plants decorate the porches of the 3200 block of Dudley Avenue, October 1, 1937. These trim, Northeast Baltimore daylight-style homes have wooden steps and face a well-tended street that could pass the inspection of the most fastidious of housekeepers.

253. The Gardenville loop of the No. 15 streetcar line filled up with transit riders the morning of July 1, 1952. The streetcars behind the fence would never arrive, however because of a transit strike.

251. Opposite, workmen tend the roof and steeple of the old St. Anthony of Padua Church, Gardenville, about 1915.

254. Berman's Market and the Shure drug store, 3101-03 Belair Road, October 1, 1937. The market offered Pillsbury flour, Ovaltine, Coca-Cola and Oxydol. A sign announces that Mayfield Avenue homes are open for inspection. Next door, the Vilma movie theater featured Loretta Young in "Love Under Fire."

255. In the Depression, the unemployed were put to work to improve Brehm's Lane, at Kenyon Avenue, in 1932.

256. Berger Avenue in Gardenville is neatly lined with the tidy homes characteristic of Northeast Baltimore, May 20, 1958.

257. The Overlea Youth Recreation Center opened with a dance December 22, 1943. Photographed were Donald Fryer, Ann Walters, Gloria Marks, Betty Wooden, Lorain Feltis and Edgar Plitt.

258. A graceful canopy of trees shades an unhurried corner of Hawthorn and Upland roads in Roland Park, April 1941. The view is north on Hawthorn, one of the oldest streets in this early planned garden suburb. Many of the soaring elm trees have died since the photo was taken. The oldest homes in this section date from the 1890s.

154

Chapter 7: NORTH

259. A wet snow in December 1942 slowed traffic at Charles Street and North Avenue. The shops include the Adolph beauty parlor, Bickford's restaurant, the Aurora movie house, Oriole Cafeteria and Tuttle's Hall, where dances were held.

260. The Food Fair chain was one of the first self-service food retailers to serve Baltimore customers. On October 31, 1935, the chain's first local store opened in the 2500 block of Greenmount Avenue. Shoppers were told "Do not bring bags or baskets. We supply them free." That opening day attracted attention as coffee sold for 23 cents a pound, a quart of shucked oysters went for 9 cents and bread was two loaves for 17 cents. The size of the market — larger than older neighborhood grocery stores — and its department store-like layout — made it a novelty.

261. The auditorium of Baltimore Polytechnic Institute, North Avenue and Barclay Street, is the background for the Baltimore Student Band assembled for a group photo in December 1938. The auditorium was demolished in 1985.

262. Dolan's saloon, 1907 Greenmount Avenue, was locally famous for its brass rail under the window and its clock. ''If that clock was wrong, we'd get 15 or 20 outraged phone calls,'' recalled owner Joe Dolan. The place closed about 1955. It had a large Irish following.

263. The June 27, 1939 Shriner's Convention was one of the largest conventions ever held in Baltimore. Here a unit of the parade that accompanied the assembly swings into North Avenue, from Howard Street, past the Oriole Pontiac showroom. ''More than one-quarter

of Baltimore's population jammed the streets for three hours," **The Sun** noted in its parade coverage the next day.

264. This May 1930 view of North Avenue looks east from Maryland Avenue to Baltimore Polytechnic Institute. Included are the North Avenue Market building, its bowling alley and shops; the Park Bank; the Sports Centre, where local ice hockey teams competed; and the Seventh Baptist Church. North Avenue was a busy streetcar crosstown route, though it was rapidly filling up with automobiles. The city's first traffic signal, a 1922 hand-operated beacon, was placed at Charles Street and North Avenue. It was automated in 1928.

265. Charles Yardley Turner, director of the Maryland Institute and a well known mural painter, is seen here criticizing the work of the summer life class at the Johns Hopkins University's Homewood campus, July 1917. Turner had recently completed several murals for Baltimore's Court House.

266. Opposite, the arrival of the canvas awning meant warm weather had arrived. These 3100 block of Guilford Avenue homes, new in 1916, are well outfitted against the summer sun. Baltimore's summers brought dark blue window blinds, straw rugs and slipcovers. This neighborhood, now known as Charles Village, was then called Peabody Heights.

160

267. On June 5, 1943, Lakewood swimming pool, 2519 North Charles Street, was crowded during a World War II boom period. The pool opened in 1932 and lasted about 20 summers. Water carnivals, beauty contests, professional wrestling matches, diving exhibitions and fashion shows were held here. The pool was larger than Olympic size and featured a stretch of beach with sand imported from Cape May, New Jersey. Lakewood was a popular gathering place. Its juke box was tuned loud and played poolside. The site later became an office building and parking lot.

268. The 26th Street Art Mart was a regular weekend fixture that stretched along the first block of East 26th Street in the 1960s.

162

269. The 3100 block of St. Paul Street, March 30, 1948, was a popular Homewood area shopping spot. Streetcar service had just ended and new buses dodged traffic along the street. Businesses included an American grocery store, a Log Cabin candy shop and an A&P.

270. The corner of 29th and St. Paul streets in 1903 was very much on the fringe of Baltimore's residential development. The photograph faces the northwest toward the house at 2900 St. Paul Street.

271. Vice President Richard M. Nixon was the guest of honor to throw out the first ball for the Orioles' major league return to Baltimore, April 15, 1954. Before the first home game, a large parade formed at University Parkway and Charles Street. The floats and marching units were led by Mr. Nixon and his wife, Pat, in an open Cadillac. The Vice President is shown here, by the University Baptist Church, with a float that contrasted the Orioles of the past with those of the future.

272. International League Oriole right fielder Glenn Chapman slides into home plate during a four-run rally in the sixth inning August 22, 1936 at Oriole Park, in the 300 block of E. 29th Street. The rally gave the Birds a commanding lead and they went on to pound the Albany Senators 18-9. Holding the bats is second baseman Max Bishop.

273. Even though Baltimore lacked a major league team, Baltimoreans were faithful to their International League Orioles. Here a crowd enters Oriole Park, in the 300 block of E. 29th Street, in the middle 1930s.

274. Baseball spectators at Oriole Park in the summer of 1940 appear formally dressed in shirts and ties.

275. The crossroads of Waverly is the corner of Greenmount Avenue and 33rd Street. The Boulevard Theatre, which opened in 1921, featured Laraine Day in "Tycoon," while "You Were Meant for Me" with Dan Dailey was the next feature. The Burriss & Kemp drug store and Schwaab's soda fountain, right, were neighborhood institutions in January 1948 when the photo was taken.

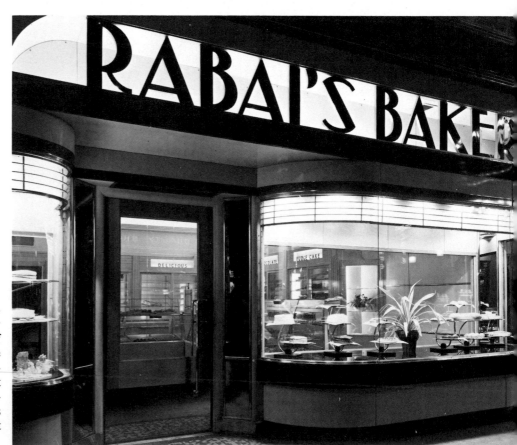

276. Louis Rabai's bakery, at 3215 Greenmount Avenue, opted for a sleek new facade in 1938. The store was just one of many shops that operated in Waverly at the time. Others included the Martha Washington, Virginia Dare and Kettle Kraft candy shops, Adler's clothing, a Woolworth, Crown dime store, Brandau's men's clothing and a White Coffee Pot restaurant.

277. Greenmount Avenue and 33rd Street was a major North Baltimore intersection. This June 1929 photograph shows the Standard Oil operation and a sign directing motorists to York and Harrisburg. Across the street was competition, a Lord Baltimore station.

278. These newly built homes with sun parlors were considered the last word in rowhouse design in the middle 1920s. The shot is of the 800 block of Venable Avenue, a street named for Major Richard M. Venable, a city parks proponent who died in 1910. Venable Park, site of the stadium, was also named for the progressive lawyer who served in the Civil War as a Confederate major.

279. The city had not yet paved Waverly's Homestead Street, between Adams and Taylor streets, on November 19, 1920. The simple frame houses and wood fences were frequently chronicled in the romantic writings of Lizette Woodworth Reese.

281. Major league baseball returned to Baltimore April 15, 1954. A newly completed Memorial Stadium was sold out as the Orioles defeated the Chicago White Sox 3 to 1. Gunther's beer had the scoreboard. Some 46,354 baseball-starved fans packed the house.

282. Loyal Baltimore Colts fans turned out in force for a game against the Green Bay Packers, October 25, 1959. The amazing Colts were then the talk of Baltimore as the team earned back-to-back world championships in 1958 and 1959.

280. Opposite, the old Baltimore Stadium occupied the site of Memorial Stadium on 33rd Street. A Shriners' Parade passes in the 1930s. Note the enterprising young sidewalk venders offering cold soft drinks. Baltimore Stadium was built in 1922 as a football bowl and could seat 80,000 on bleacher seats. Navy-Notre Dame games were played here during the period.

283. Bretton Place, Guilford, designed by residential architect Edward L. Palmer, was opened for sale in the spring of 1916. The homes were among the first properties constructed in the community. "Here skillful architecture and landscape gardening will combine with the beauty of nature and the wise planning of broadminded men, who are not afraid to do things in the large way. Guilford will be their monument," noted some promotional material of the same period the photograph was taken.

284. Baltimore architect John Ahlers once said that it took him less than half an hour to make a design sketch for a home for Dr. and Mrs. George L. Streeter at 3707 St. Paul Street in late 1936. The house was completed in April 1937 and captured serveral architectural awards. It was the first modern-design home in Guilford. The glass-block windows were such a novelty that the residence was opened to the public for a 10-cent admission fee.

285. Bedford Square, in Guilford, is the name given to the point where St. Paul Street joins Charles Street. From 1916 until 1946, it was also a streetcar terminal and waiting room. The No. 1 trolley car, right, was in regular service. The car at the left, 5201, is a special chartered car for a rail fans' trip. The photo was taken in 1946, shortly before the St. Paul Street tracks were taken up and the route converted to bus service. The Bedford Square waiting station survives.

286. An outdoor mass was celebrated on the porch of the faculty residence of Loyola College, Evergreen, September 10, 1922, as the Jesuit school was moving to its Charles Street and Cold Spring Lane campus. The house was constructed in 1895-6 as the residence of Horatio Whitridge Garrett. Loyola College was founded in 1855 and operated for nearly 70 years in the 700 block of N. Calvert Street.

287. A May procession at Notre Dame of Maryland called for religious banners and white dresses in the 1920s. The school, founded in 1873 by the School Sisters of Notre Dame, then included an elementary and high school and college. It is now known as the College of Notre Dame of Maryland, 4701 North Charles Street.

289. Opposite, this magazine-perfect scene at Springlake Way, at the corner of St. Dunstan's Road, Homeland, 1938, sums up what the Roland Park Company tried to achieve in its residential development. A year later the firm explained its control: ''The fact that all plans have to pass a severe test on the part of the Roland Park Company's architectural committee prevents freakish, or even extreme manifestations of taste, not only in regard to lines and mass but color.''

288. The Springlake Way lakes in Homeland were the ideal setting for ice skating and informal ice hockey, January 10, 1940. The ornamental ponds dated from 1843 when David Perine, Homeland's owner, had them dug. They were fed by springs. Homeland had been a private estate which the city once considered for a public park. In 1924 the estate was sold to the Roland Park Company, which carefully developed it as a planned residential community.

291. York Road, looking south from Bellona Avenue, had the look of a village September 29, 1909. Govans was then a Baltimore County community. The patriotic celebration was occasioned by the completion of a new system of fire hydrants connected by underground pipes. Many notables attended and every house on York road was bedecked with Japanese lanterns and flags. A delegation of the city's finest mounted police passes in the late afternoon following a long parade. Firecrackers and fireworks exploded that evening, but no actual fires tested the new system.

292. Hochschild, Kohn & Company's York Road and Belvedere Avenue department store opened September 28, 1948. Max Hochschild, the firm's 93-year-old founder, cut the ribbon as 2,000 shoppers swarmed into the new suburban branch. The branch lasted 35 years here before it was closed and the building converted to other retail and office uses. This photo was taken July 7, 1950.

174

293. The 700 block of McCabe Avenue, Govans, was invitingly outfitted with canvas awnings and hydrangea bushes in June 1958.

294. Recess time at the Blessed Sacrament School, 4101 Old York Road, May 22, 1961, found children and their spiritual director in the school's play yard.

175

295. Looking east on 36th Street, from Falls Road, Hampden, May 6, 1958. This is the Avenue. A No. 10 trackless trolley is headed into this scene.

296. A road construction gang repairs Falls Road at the Mount Vernon mills, September 24, 1922. The Jones Falls provided water power to textile mills in this valley. The mill buildings date from 1873, 1879 and 1881. They are surrounded by a village of stone mill workers' houses and a cotton house where bales of cotton were stored as they awaited processing.

297. A 1930s interior view of the Pratt Library's Branch 7 in Hampden, shows its reading room. Note the oil painting. The branch, at Falls Road, 3641 Falls Road, was donated by foundry owner Robert Poole, whose home, Maple Hill, was located just across the street. Poole also directed that the branch would be built with a room to be used by the Provident Savings Bank. He liked to encourage thrift and learning.

298. Children from the Hampden elementary school, No. 55, visit Engine Company 21, 3724 Roland Avenue, in the middle 1920s.

177

299. The presence of a steam shovel digging a foundation for the Bank of Hampden, at the northeast corner of 36th Street and Roland Avenue, 1924, was a neighborhood occasion. The building later became Sandler's department store.

300. The Baltimore Country Club, Roland Park, featured grass tennis courts. The club was organized in the 1890s and brought golf to Baltimore. The game was then so unknown that the equipment had to be imported from Scotland. The photograph, which dates from the 1920s, shows a tennis match being watched by a considerable gathering of spectators.

301. Streetcar tracks ran down the center of University Parkway from 1908 through the middle 1940s. The University Apartments and a corner of the Christian Science Church are at the right in the early 1920s. The Johns Hopkins Homewood campus is on the left.

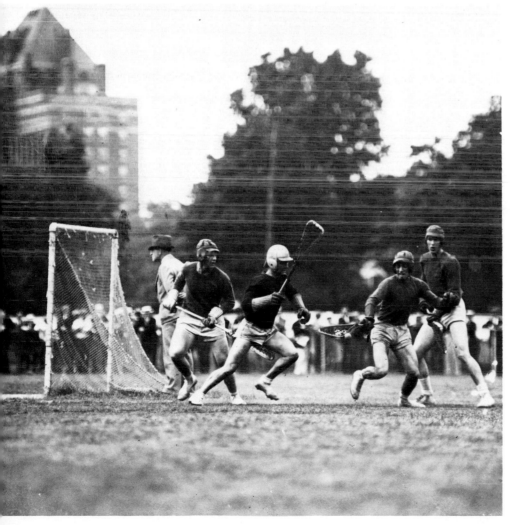

302. Spring arrives in Baltimore with the lacrosse season. Shown here is Johns Hopkins lacrosse action, 1929, on Homewood Field at University Parkway. The school was founded in 1876 and originally had a downtown campus with buildings scattered along Howard and Eutaw streets. By the 1910s Hopkins began building a new campus at Homewood in North Baltimore. Constructing Homewood Field was a priority because the school had no room for outdoor athletics downtown.

179

303. The Maryland and Pennsylvania Railroad used the Stony Run Valley on its roundabout route to York, Pennsylvania from Falls Road. Here the Ma & Pa's afternoon mail steams along near Cold Spring Lane about 1900.

304. Baltimore engineer Wendel Bollman obtained a patent for a truss bridge, which was fabricated for use across the country. In 1886 one of his spans crossed Lake Roland, part of the city's water supply system.

305. The Olmsted Brothers, the highly regarded landscape architects, designed the streets and contours of the west side of Roland Park, including this portion of Longwood Road, shown here about 1915. The section of the neighborhood slopes into the Jones Falls Valley and is known for its foliage and hilly terrain. Local architects designed the residences.

306. The soda fountain staff of the Morgan Millard drug store and soda fountain stands at attention at the Roland Park Shopping Center in 1979. The center is considered one of the first in this country. Finished in 1896, the block of Tudor-style stores and offices was surrounded by trolley tracks linking the garden suburb with the city. Roland Park, a neighborhood of winding streets and rambling single homes, is one of the country's early planned communities. Its first section was designed by engineer George E. Kessler, with later sections designed by landscape architect Frederick Law Olmsted Jr.

307. Billy Beardsley, son of Grace and Wilfred Beardsley, who both taught language at Goucher College, stands by displays of books written by Roland Park residents. The elder Beardsleys, as well as authors M.B. Croker, Swepson Earle, Robert Hegner, O.E. Janney, H.S. Jennings, Anna I. Miller, L. Wardlaw Miles, A.O. Overbeck, George Partridge, Frederick Stieff and J.S. Strange all contributed copies of their books to the Pratt's Roland Park branch in November 1935.

309. **Opposite,** the view of Roland Avenue and Cold Spring Lane looks south on Roland Avenue, November 11, 1932. In the distance is the water tower, built in 1909, which stored water for Hampden and Woodberry residents. Roland Park maintained its own water supply system.

308. The forty-second annual commencement and Founder's Day ceremonies were held at Gilman School, June 12, 1939. Dr. Isaiah Bowman, president of the Johns Hopkins University, gave the address.

Appendix A: THE FOUNDER

Enoch Pratt, born September 10, 1808, had the Yankee gift for making money. He arrived in Baltimore from his native Massachusetts with $150. He said he worked by "the plain, New England way of doing things." The philosophy was successful. He was a rich man by the time he was 40.

His introduction to giving away money wisely came from George Peabody, who named him the treasurer of the newly founded Peabody Institute. Pratt held the post for for 35 years. During Baltimore's hot summer months, when many Peabody trustees fled the city, Enoch Pratt remained at his desk, going over receipts for every penny spent.

Acting without fanfare, Pratt bought property along Mulberry Street and proceeded to have it excavated for a public library. It was not until January 1882 that he publicly announced his intention to the city government. Pratt put up about a quarter of a million dollars for this main building and four branches in city neighborhoods. Good businessman that he was, he stipulated that the city must support his effort. In striking his agreement with the city, he made the city contribute $50,000 annually. To this he added an $833,333.33 endowment, which he figured would produce another $50,000 in annual income for the library. The old Central Library opened to the public January 5, 1886.

As word of Pratt's generosity spread, his library became the model for industrialist Andrew Carnegie's philanthropy. Carnegie visited Pratt and donated much of his fortune to establish libraries in other American cities. The Carnegie Endowment also remembered Pratt, and Baltimore, by giving $500,000 for Pratt neighborhood branch libraries.

Enoch Pratt lived to see his dream. When asked about his long years of good health, he replied, "went to parties, danced, played cards, and drank all the champagne that anyone else paid for." He died September 17, 1896.

310. Opposite, Enoch Pratt stands with other members of his iron firm at its counting rooms on Charles Street, just south of Baltimore, about 1890. The building was destroyed in the 1904 fire.

Appendix B: THE PRATT SYSTEM

There is no section of Baltimore that Pratt libraries have not served. As populations shifted, the library system has adjusted to serve the people. This list of Pratt agencies details this service. Branches are listed by their number.

Central Library

Central Library opened February 3, 1933 at 400 Cathedral Street. The building was six years in planning and, upon completion, was hailed as the model city library. It was the creation of Joseph L. Wheeler, Pratt's third librarian, who proved that a great library building could be a "thing of beauty" as well as a "sensible convenience."

The architects were Edward Lippincott Tilton and Alfred Morton Githens of New York and Clyde and Nelson Friz of Baltimore. In charging the designers, Wheeler asked for a building that would "depart from traditional institutionalism of the past." He wanted no mausoleum. But he wanted the dignity "befitting such an institution, . . . a dignity characterized by friendliness rather than aloofness." Wheeler described the results as a bright and lively interior distinctly refreshing and inspiring."

More than one person noted the library had no front steps to deter mothers with baby carriages. And many a Baltimorean has been drawn into the building because of a colorful display in one of the 12 department store windows that stretch along Cathedral Street.

Wheeler believed in serving his patrons with an open floor plan wherein all departments opened to a naturally lighted Central Hall. He wanted the public to use the building without confusion.

The building materials used included marble, walnut woodwork, furniture and cabinetry, decorated brass, and a terrazzo floor. The high ceilings were often covered with eye-catching wall frescoes. In general, there was much attention given to exquisite detail work.

Occupying a place of high honor above the gates to the south end of the Central Hall is a painting of Johann Gutenberg, the man who invented movable type. Opposite him on the north end is William Caxton, the first English printer, presenting a copy of his first book to his patroness, Marguerite of Burgundy. On the lower east and west walls are portraits of the Lords Baltimore. They belonged to Dr. Hugh H. Young, the Baltimore surgeon who agreed to donate them to the Pratt provided its trustees purchase another portrait, that the of the second Lord Baltimore, from William Randolph Hearst.

A ground floor Children's Department, with its own garden entrance off Mulberry Street, has been praised and affectionately remembered by its patrons. "Our beautiful new Children's Room ranked for a while with the seven wonders of the world. People came to admire the courtyard beyond the great bay window, the fish pool, the decorated ceiling and the firescreen ornamented with friendly looking dragons," noted librarian Elizabeth Hart. The iron firescreen was the work of Baltimore ironmonger Victor Weisberger, who also forged the andirons and fire tools in the Edgar Allan Poe Room.

Branch 1, Pitcher Street, 1886-1957

Branch 1, at Fremont Avenue and Pitcher Street, opened March 15, 1886. Richard Hart, Enoch Pratt's biographer, wrote in 1935, "Miss Mary Robb, the first librarian of Branch 1, . . . tells this story of an infant oak tree that sprouted from an acorn planted by the janitor on the lawn before the library. When the sapling was about two feet high, Miss Robb decided to dignify it with the name of Enoch Pratt. Dr. Steiner (the first librarian-in-chief) got wind of this informal Arbor Day and decided to visit the branch for the occasion. Mr. Pratt heard of 'it at the last minute, and, deserting business, drove out Fremont Street in hot haste. After a ceremony that must have been a source of considerable wonder to the neighborhood, Mr. Pratt remained on the lawn in silence, staring at the tree. Finally he said, 'Miss Robb, your oak has five branches but I haven't any.'

"The angel that watches over such awkward moments must have descended to the lady's aid. 'But Mr. Pratt,' she objected smiling, 'you have five branches.' . . . Mr. Pratt's thin lips expanded to a broad grin. 'Thank you, Miss Robb, so I have . . . so I have.' "

The branch closed March 15, 1957 after precisely 71 years of service. Converted to other uses, the building still stands. It was designed by architect Charles L. Carson, who was responsible for the first six branch libraries.

Branch 2, Hollins Street, 1886-1964
Hollins Payson, 1964-

The first Branch 2, Calhoun and Hollins streets, opened March 8, 1886. Librarian Alice Gerber, writing in 1926, noted that the branch was most heavily patronized on market days, when the nearby Hollins Market was so busy. H.L. Mencken used this branch as a young scholar and remarked in his "Heathen Days,": "Between them (two teachers at Polytechnic Institute) they converted me into one of the most assiduous customers that the Enoch Pratt Free Library in Baltimore has had in its whole history. There were winters when I visited it almost every weekday, and before I began to be fetched by the literary movement of the nineties I had read half the classical English repertoire."

The replacement Branch 2, Hollins-Payson, 31 South Payson Street, was dedicated June 8, 1964 at an open house. Public service began the next day. The branch was described as "contemporary in design . . . of light brick with annodized aluminum door and window frames and natural redwood sunshades . . . planned to harmonize with older neighborhood features" It was designed by architects Jewell and Wolf. Its entrance contains the Mencken quotation: "No man can get anywhere in this world in any really worthy and endurable manner without some recourse to books."

"New assistants at the branch found street names — plus Southwest Baltimore pronunciation — an added handicap in registration. Who, outside this area, would dream that 'CATH-A-REEN' Street' is spelled like 'Catharine'? . . . One mother called up to protest that the librarian said her child didn't know where she lived," wrote Fern E. Stowe of the first busy week at Hollins-Payson, when thousands of children registered for cards.

Branch 3, Light Street, 1886-1971
New Light Street, 1971-

Branch 3, Light and Gittings streets, opened February 27, 1886. This was the third Enoch Pratt's donated neighborhood branches. In 1908 the branch was still illuminated by gas lights, causing librarians to complain that it was difficult to read the titles of shelved books. Electricity did not arrive until the early 1920s.

The library was once the scene of a neighborhood bombing. On the evening of December 27, 1937, six boys were asked to leave by librarian Mary M. Diddle because they were disturbing patrons. They took revenge by visiting the Hanover Market, picking up discarded grapefruit, tomatoes and other garbage, then returning to pelt the library and break a window. They were charged with disorderly conduct.

The old Light Street Branch survived the fruit bombing and served until August 20, 1971 when the old structure was permanently closed. About a year before, construction had begun on a replacement branch which opened to the public on September 1, 1971. Located at Light and Ostend streets, it was a new building designed by Fryer and Associates. Peter Van Rossum executed a distinctive brick relief sculpture on the facade.

Branch 4, Canton, 1886-

The Canton branch, Ellwood Avenue and O'Donnell Street, opened February 15, 1886. While Enoch Pratt donated the building, the Canton Company gave the land. In 1879, Pratt served on the board of Canton's Workingmen's Institute, a combined reading room and small museum founded by the Rev. J. Wynne Jones, pastor of the Canton Methodist Church. Pratt, whose iron firm was located nearby, was duly impressed by Canton residents' reading habits. The success of the Workingmen's Institute confirmed Pratt's intentions to found a library system.

Martin C. McMahon, who resided at 207 Curley Street, wrote of the Canton branch, "I was fortunate that I had a mother who loved to read. I was further helped along in my good reading habits by the librarians. . . . Miss Emma G. Mills was the head librarian at Branch 4. She resided in the 3100 block of Fleet Street.

"She was a censor before I knew what the word meant. You could pick out a book, take it to the desk and have a card and book stamped. If she thought it was a book that was not right for innocent eyes, she merely took it, put it under the desk and told you it was not for you to read. There was no redress; that was it. No talk could change her mind. If you wanted a book, you had better go and select another. Bring it back and she would say, 'Now that is more like it.' There was no use in saying anything to my mother. She would, like all the other parents, agree with Miss Mills. There was another librarian — Miss Sarah Garrity who lived on North Wolfe Street — who was along the same lines as Miss Mills. They were both fine women who had their jobs and the interests of the people they dealt with at heart."

Miss Mills, who began with Pratt in 1907, came to Canton in 1910 and remained there until her retirement in 1947. She was a keen observer of the neighborhood. When patronage began to fall off in the 1920s, she linked the change to O'Donnell Street's decline as a business street. "The trade belt has shifted north about six blocks and east about three." She advised her library superiors to purchase more appealing children's books printed in bright colors as a way of drawing young readers back to the Canton.

In 1984 the Canton Improvement Association spearheaded a successful drive to restore the building to its original appearance. A neat iron fence, landscaping and historic marker were also added.

Branch 5, Broadway, 1886-1971
New Branch 5, 1971-

Branch 5, North Broadway and Miller Street, opened in 1888, using the same plans as the first four branches. The branch served Johns Hopkins Hospital, Church Home, old Sinai and other hospitals, as well as many Bohemian immigrant families. The building continued in use until the new branch 5, Broadway and Orleans Street, opened February 1, 1971. It was designed by Morris H. Steinhorn. A steel sculptural column was designed by Roger Majorowicz to stand in front of the building.

Branch 6, Peabody Heights, 1896-

The Peabody Heights (Charles Village) branch, 2521 St. Paul Street, opened November 14, 1896 with 6,500 books. The architect was Charles L. Carson. Enoch Pratt, who died as the branch was opening, donated the land, bought in March 1896, and building. At the very end of his life he was still supervising its interior and furnishings. The branch was popular with Goucher College students, whose campus was then only a few blocks south. In 1906 a lot in the rear was purchased, to be enclosed and a lawn and garden planted. Each spring cut flowers began appearing on the desks and tables. Electricity replaced gas lights in 1920.

Librarians noted many changes in this neighborhood over the years. They watched the old homes being converted into apartments and business offices. They watched patronage decline as the new Central opened in 1933, but still had a steady stream of students using Branch 6. During the 1940s, Pratt officials considered closing it and building a larger library at North Avenue and Calvert Street. Instead, Branch 6 was renovated in 1952 and that year librarian Anna L. Kehoe watched creeping electronic competition on Saturdays: "The afternoon business is brisk (at No. 6), but it dwindles off to nothing in the evening so that the branch now resembles a morgue on this night. Could it be due to the better television shows on this evening?"

311. Joseph Wheeler, Pratt's director from 1926-1945, never tired of promoting books and the library.

312. Architect Charles Carson's rendering for the model of the first six branches.

Branch 7, Hampden, 1900-

Branch 7, the Hampden branch, 3611 Falls Road, opened July 2, 1900. Robert Poole, who owned the large iron foundry that was one of the major employers in the industrialized Hampden-Woodberry community, gave the site and building. He had been the chief supporter of a free circulating library organized about 1885 for Woodberry residents. The incorporators of the Woodberry Free Reading Rooms and Circulating Library included T. Harrison Garrett, German H. Hunt, Robert and George Poole and J. Morrison Harris. Charles M. White, the principal of Woodberry High School, served as librarian. In 1887, there were 174 male and 460 female card holders.

In deference to Poole's wishes, an agreement was made between Pratt and the Provident Savings Bank for the bank to rent a one-room branch office. The bank remained until 1915. The building departed in architectural style from earlier Pratt branches. It was of the Colonial Revival style and its architect was Joseph Evans Sperry, who would be called upon to design several other libraries.

Patronage at the branch was directly connected to labor conditions in the community. When the cotton duck mills in the Jones Falls Valley were working less, the library was more crowded with unemployed mill hands. In 1909, the librarian noted: "Owing to a bowling alley, pool room and moving picture show which have recently been opened in ths neighborhood, quite a number of our readers and patrons have deserted the branch in the evening, finding these places more attractive."

Librarian Anna L. Kehoe wrote in her 1957 report on this branch: "Television and movies promote more demand for recreational reading . . . It was a real hard blow to several men patrons to learn that Matt Dillon was not a real person."

Branch 8, Walbrook, 1903, 1907-1957 New Walbrook, 1957-

Branch 8, the Walbrook branch, has a long history. In the 1890s, Pratt first dispatched boxes of books to a public school in Walbrook, an early suburban community. When the school needed the space occupied by the books, Pratt took over a streetcar waiting shed January 2, 1903. Real estate developer Francis A. White offered the library a well built frame structure which had been constructed as the Union Chapel for the use of Protestant denominations. It was the first public building in Walbrook. Located at Clifton Avenue and Hilton Street, the chapel was converted and opened as a library September 3, 1907. It was enlarged in 1921 by architect Thomas Machen.

Walbrook librarian Mary K.C. Thomason wrote in 1926, "At Branch 8 we have been obliged to be real salesmen and have had to work much harder for our book circulation than the neighborhoods where there has always been greater circulation."

Churchgoers continued to confuse the library with a house of worship for many years thereafter. However, members of the Daily Bible Vacation School of the Temple Baptist Church took up a collection in 1943 and bought Branch 8 an electric sign reading "Library." It helped stop the confusion.

A new Branch 8, 3203 West North Avenue, was dedicated April 14, 1957. This modern structure was designed by Finney, Dodson, Smeallie & Associates. Public service began the next day.

Branch 9, Locust Point, 1900-1957

The old Locust Point branch, began about 1900 as a book delivery room in a Hull Street store. In December 1901, the Pratt made a lending-service agreement with the Locust Point Settlement, a settlement house operated at 1504 Fort Avenue. When Andrew Carnegie's funds became available for branch construction, the Baltimore and Ohio Railroad donated a library site at Towson and Beason streets. The lot was conveyed to the city June 16, 1909. Ground was broken in March 1910 and Branch 9 was formally dedicated October 15, 1910. Its architect was Joseph Evans Sperry.

That year a German gentleman visited the new branch. He had not used his card for two years and explained to the librarian, "I did not know I could get German books from the library until *mein Sohn* told me that the library lady had been getting them for him." The patron continued to return, week after week.

In September 1926 Locust Point librarian Blanche A. Moffatt noted more children were using the library that fall because their mothers were not engaged in seasonal canning factory work. When the mothers worked, she explained, the children were made to stay home and perform the housework. By December of that year, she wrote that the Locust Point branch was at its busiest in the evening: "Between the rush hours of 6 to 9 p.m. it is almost impossible to perform desk and police duties at the same time."

By 1928 the neighborhood, led by school principal Persis K. Miller and the Pratt staff concurred that Locust Point would be better served if the branch were transferred to School No. 76, the Francis Scott Key School, Fort Avenue and Decatur Street. It remained there until the branch closed in June 1957.

Branch 9, Waverly, 1971-

A new Waverly branch, 33rd and Barclay streets, opened April 22, 1971. It was designed by architects Rogers and Vaeth. Located near the Greemount Avenue and 33rd Street neighborhood crossroads, it has become one of the busier branches in the Pratt system. The branch is a contemporary, one-level building. Sculptor Thomas E. Hoffmaster Jr. created a welded steel piece that portrays a series of figures associated with the book world — Edgar Allan Poe, H.L. Mencken, Cyrano

de Bergerac, Long John Silver, "Charlotte's Web," Alice in Wonderland, Humpty-Dumpty, Frederick Douglass and Tom Sawyer. A woodcut depicting old Waverly, from Lizette Woodworth Reese's "A Victorian Village," also hangs in the branch.

Branch 10, Oldtown, 1902-1938

Branch Ten served Oldtown residents in rented rooms. In 1902 the Pratt trustees found themselves with two pleasant offers. The women members of the Arundell Good Government Club offered funds for rent, heat, light and janitor's service for a library station. About the same time the officers of the Provident Savings Bank notified the Pratt that a room in their new Gay and Mott streets branch bank was available. The Oldtown Merchants' and Manufacturers' Association was among city groups asking for library service. Accordingly, Branch 10 opened October 6, 1902.

The small branch was an immediate hit. "The children expect the librarian to show them the latest stitches in embroidery, to help in translating their Latin and to decide which was the greater in fame, George Washington or Abraham Lincoln. . . . It is nothing unusual to treat burns and cuts," noted the library's annual report for 1902.

This was one of the first branches to

experiment with shelves open to the public. The Pratt administration was hesitant to accept public access to all books and became skeptical when some 15 volumes failed to show up during an inventory. But the public liked the idea. In 1928 the branch moved to 622 Aisquith Street, at Gay. When the branch closed permanently December 31, 1938, about 100 books had not been returned. Among the missing titles were "David Copperfield" and "Gone with the Wind." The Oldtown Merchants' and Manufacturers' Association protested the closing and presented the city's Board of Estimates with a petition containing 4,000 signatures, but the neighborhood had lost population due to street widenings. Book circulation was also in a decline. The opening of the Orleans Street Viaduct in 1935 perhaps did the most to change the neighborhood. This elevated highway linked Oldtown with Franklin Street and the new Central Library, which Oldtown residents found served their needs better than did the one-room Branch 10.

Branch 10, Northwood, 1960-

The Northwood branch, 4420 Loch Raven Boulevard, was dedicated April 20, 1960. The site was donated by Mr. and Mrs. Milton Schwaber, who developed a shopping center adjacent to the site. City voters

313. An old community church became the Walbrook branch, shown here in 1917.

approved the construction cost. Architects Smith and Veale designed the building. Mayor Thomas J. D'Alesandro Jr. and other officials broke ground for the building October 16, 1958.

Branch 11, Central Avenue, 1904-1960
Branch 11, Central Avenue and Watson Street, opened November 23, 1921. The architects were Archer and Allen. The branch's history was intertwined with the Eastern European immigrant community that settled here. "Preponderantly Jewish by faith, the newcomers were isolated from their new country, and to some extent by each other, by diverse languages and local traditions," wrote Wayne E. Jackl in a 1972 article. The first Pratt Station No. 11 was financially underwritten by the Maccabeans, a philanthropic group that earlier had established the Maccabean House, a settlement house in the neighborhood. Housed in a rented room, the library station opened December 14, 1904. "Activity at Station No. 11 . . . peaked in 1914 when it circulated 52,030 books, over 6,000 more than any other Pratt agency except Central library," Jackl noted. World War I and other complications postponed permanent branch construction for several more frustrating years. The building, which still stands, closed in January 1960.

314. Patrons fill the Waverly branch, opening day, April 22, 1971.

Branch 12, Mount Clare, 1909-1960
The Mount Clare branch, Barre and Carroll (St. Peter) streets, opened May 22, 1909, although the library had an earlier station on Washington Boulevard. This was the first branch built with Andrew Carnegie's funds. A library building committee had visited Pittsburgh, Philadelphia and Cleveland to inspect modern library systems and to get fresh ideas. Architect Joseph Evans Sperry got the commission for the job.

On hand for the Mount Clare dedication were Pratt trustees James A. Gary, Charles J. Bonaparte and Baltimore's Mayor Barry Mahool. Thomas J. Hayward, of the firm of Bartlett, Hayward & Company, the iron foundry that was a major employer in Southwest Baltimore, donated funds for the site.

The building was hailed because its books were all stored on open shelves within public reach. The building was also the first branch with a public meeting room, which doubled as a lecture hall and book discussion area. Trustees ruled, however, that no tobacco could be used in this room. The branch was constructed of a yellowish-brown brick and trimmed with Kibbe stone. The interior had quartered oak. Because of the ethnic composition of

the neighborhood, the Mount Clare branch often had requests for books in German and Lithuanian. The branch closed in January 1960.

Branch 13, Patterson Park, 1910-
The Patterson Park branch, Linwood Avenue and Fayette streets, opened amid considerable public ceremony April 9, 1910. The architect was Joseph Evans Sperry. It was an Andrew Carnegie gift and the Park Board supplied the land. Members of the East End Improvement Association cheered as the building opened. The Pratt trustees and officials then posed to be photographed by **The Baltimore American.** Original plans called for the branch to have been located in the Patterson Park Casino.

Architect Sperry visited Florence, Italy in 1906. He recommended that Branch 13 should contain three reproduction casts from the Singing Gallery of the Florence Cathedral. The casts were made from originals by Luca della Robbia, the Italian sculptor. The panels depict boys and girls singing and playing musical instruments. "I selected (the casts) from the collection in the shop of the Casteras Brothers in New York on account of its beauty of lines and modelling," he said.

It was not long before this branch became busy with patrons from the new rowhouses going up in East Baltimore. Librarians reported the community was heavily Catholic. By 1940 a set of "The Catholic Encyclopedia" had been consulted so often, it needed complete rebinding. During World War II the branch was busy with Glenn L. Martin Company workers who found the library convenient to the corner where their shuttle bus picked up and deposited them. Several of the branch's best readers who joined the military wrote back to the librarians while stationed overseas. The branch was enlarged in 1954.

Branch 14, Forest Park, 1910-
The Forest Park branch, Garrison Boulevard and Calloway Avenue, was dedicated November 26, 1910. Exactly four years earlier, November 26, 1906, a neighborhood meeting called by the Forest Park Improvement Association was held at St. Mark's Methodist Church to urge Pratt trustees to consider a site in that community for a branch. In October 1909 some ten architects were asked to join in a design competition for a Forest Park branch.

Architects Ellicott and Emmart won the competition. Work began the following

191

315. Andrew Carnegie's donation built the handsome Forest Park Branch.

April and the building was paid for with Andrew Carnegie funds. The city had previously owned the land. The branch contained a room where the Women's Club of Forest Park held its regular meetings. The Forest Park Improvement Association annually decorated the branch for July 4th with 200 Japanese lanterns and numerous American flags. When the branch was remodeled and enlarged in August 1954, the architect was Frederick A. Fletcher.

Novelist and television executive Robert Kotlowitz paid tribute to the Forest Park branch: ''I can say that the presence of Branch 14 on Garrison Boulevard and its accessibility to the community — meaning me between the ages of eight and sixteen — was one of the great formative experiences of my life. The library and its books were for me a page-by-page unfolding of the world outside Forest Park and it was perhaps the single most potent cultural force in the community to help satisfy my greed. The chief librarian . . . encouraged me always and provided me an environment of well being and benign welcome that I will never forget.''

Branch 15, Homestead, 1911-1975
The Homestead (Waverly) branch, 1443 Gorsuch Avenue, opened in December 9, 1911. The architects were Archer and Allen. The branch was an Andrew Carne-

gie gift. The land was donated by Scott Carswell in memory of Robert W. Carswell. It became a library center in 1970 and closed in December 1975.

Branch 16, Keyworth Avenue, 1912-
Branch 16, 2610 Keyworth Avenue near Park Heights Avenue, was dedicated September 28, 1912 in the presence of many residents. Clarence W. Perkins said at that ceremony, ''We have progressed very much in this neighborhood in the past ten years. In 1900 one could only count about 40 houses from Fulton Avenue, while now there are 500.''

Branch 16's architects were J. Appleton Wilson and Wilson L. Smith. The land was given by H.C. and W.W. Shirley in memory of their parents, William and Ellen Frazier Shirley. William Shirley was born in London in 1816 and moved to Baltimore in 1834. He spent his professional life in the crockery business. In 1852 he purchased a large tract of Northwest Baltimore land and was instrumental in the opening of Park Heights Avenue. He was also president of the horse car transit line which ran along the street. He died in 1900, but his children continued to reside in the neighborhood. Both public School 59, the Louisa May Alcott Elementary School, and the Keyworth Avenue Branch 16 were built on William Shirley's land. In the branch's early years, librarians noted

that book requests often rose in the summer, a time when circulation normally lags. The readers were seasonal residents of Northwest Baltimore's summer hotels and boarding houses.

Branch 17, Easterwood, 1914-1953
The Easterwood Park branch, 2217 W. North Avenue, was dedicated June 26, 1914. The architect was John Appleton Wilson. The land was donated in memory of Gay Street department store owner Leon Lauer by his widow. Andrew Carnegie donated the building. It closed in January 1953.

Branch 17, Pennsylvania and North 1953-
Branch 17, North and Pennsylvania avenues, opened for public use January 15, 1953. The modern building's opening ceremonies January 14 attracted 1,500 people. The brick-and-limestone structure was designed by architects Smith and Veale. The voters approved the land and construction cost as part of a post-war librarian loan designed to place new branches in strategic, well trafficked neighborhood sites.

Dr. Joseph L. Wheeler, former Pratt director, was among the guests at the opening ceremony. He said, ''It's the finest public library (branch) in the country. It has the rest of them backed off the boards.'' The branch's expansive plate-glass windows and use of light were hailed by architectural magazines.

Branch 18, Clifton Park, 1916-
The Clifton branch, 2001 Wolfe Street, was dedicated November 16, 1916 by Mayor James Preston. At the ceremony he advised the assembled 200 children to look upon books as their best friends. The Clifton branch had serious competition from its namesake, Clifton Park. Librarian Sarah A. Gerahty complained in 1926 of the summer circulation slump. "The three sources of distraction," she said, "are the Clifton Park swimming pool, the playground and athletic field and the Friday night band concerts.''

The branch's architect was Otto G. Simonson. In the spring of 1916, Baltimore rowhouse builder Frank Novak offered the Wolfe Street land in the name of himself and his wife Florence. Novak built thousands of East and Northeast Baltimore homes. Kavon Avenue, Novak spelled backwards, is named for him. In November 1958 an addition was built on this branch to house the bookmobile's office and garage.

Branch 19, Fells Point, 1922-
The Fells Point branch, 606-610 South Ann Street, was dedicated April 21, 1922. The building was an Andrew Carnegie donation; land was donated by William H. Grafflin and the Children's Playground Association, with city assistance. The architects were Ellicott and Emmart, who managed to design an elegant branch tucked in around rowhouses. The architects created a distinctive iron gate and entrance lantern.

In 1950 librarian Sara L. Siebert opened a library stall in the nearby Broadway Market. Each Friday morning that summer, she and her staff marched across Aliceanna Street with books, pamphlets, magazines and signs. Patrons sought books on everything from crocheting to applying formstone. She even held impromptu story hours at the library stall.

"When you walk through the doors of the Fells Point Branch of the Pratt Library you enter one of the few remaining examples of a Carnegie Branch. These were neighborhood libraries endowed by philanthropist Andrew Carnegie. Over the years the term Carnegie branch has acquired other meanings. It has become associated with a particular style of architecture. In scale with the community — solid, functional, with large windows and high ceilings, the dull patina of old wood, the slightly institutional odor of numerous

316. Department store windows figured in Branch 17's design.

coats of floor wax,'' noted an editorial in the **Library Times**, a Fells Point publication honoring Branch 19 on its 60th anniversary.

Branch 20, Hamilton, 1920-1959, 1959-
The Hamilton branch, Hamilton and Richard Avenue, opened December 15, 1920. The architect was Theodore Wells Pietsch. The Hamilton Improvement Association donated the land and the building was an Andrew Carnegie gift. Librarian Laura V. Bishop, writing in 1926, noted "There is but one streetcar line out here and that is a one-man trolley from Carney to Hamilton Avenue . . . very few of the side streets are paved and walking is very bad, especially in winter." But a World War II housing boom produced many Hamilton library patrons. By the 1950s the original building was not large enough for the demands placed upon it.

A new and larger Branch 20, Harford Road and Glenmore Avenue, was designed by architects Cochran, Stephenson and Wing. It opened January 10, 1959, but only after lengthy negotiations regarding the paint specifications used in coating the steel shelving.

Branch 21, Mt. Washington, 1921-1951
Branch 21, the Mount Washington branch, Smith and Greely avenues, opened January 5, 1921. The architect was Edward H. Glidden. The land was donated by the family of John M. Carter. The branch was the subject of a heated debate from 1948-1951, when the Pratt trustees wanted to turn the building over to the city for public school use. "Hell hath no fury like a

Mount Washingtonian battling for his library,'' noted a **Sun** editorial about the community's effort to keep the library open. The trustees won out and the building closed February 17, 1951. Book service was supplied by bookmobile.

Branch 21, Pimlico, 1952-
A new Branch 21, the Pimlico branch, Park Heights and Garrison avenues, opened November 1, 1952. The land and the building were approved by city voters. **The Baltimore American** reported, "An enthusiastic crowd of howling, shoving youngsters almost spoiled the dedication ceremonies . . . But Mayor D'Alesandro saved the day by letting the children spend their enthusiasm by shouting their approval of the library loan." It took a policeman's whistle to finally quiet the group, described as the largest ever to attend a branch opening.

"Our public is drawn from every walk of life . . . nurses, housewives, students, horse breeders and stray drunks from the race track. There is an excitement and an aliveness rarely found in a library,'' noted librarian Violet F. Myer in 1952. So heavily used was the branch that some 62 patrons had all reserved copies of John Steinbeck's "East of Eden" shortly after the branch opened.

Branch 22, Govans, 1921-
Branch 22, 5714 Bellona Avenue, opened September 13, 1921, after nearly 20 years of campaigning by the Woman's Club of Govans. Long before this community was part of Baltimore city, the group established a small circulating library. It func-

tioned until World War I, when the books were distributed in military camps. In 1919, through the efforts of Mrs. C. Albert Kuper, chairman of the Neighborhood Improvement Club committee, money was being raised to purchase a lot for a Pratt Library branch.

Before the amount was raised, E. Glenn Perine donated the Bellona Avenue land. The earlier subscribers were reimbursed and the Pratt trustees agreed to build. Excavation began in early February 1921. Perine, then 96 years old, was the first to register for a card on opening day. The architects were Sill, Buckler and Fenhagen. The library was enlarged and reopened November 15, 1942.

Branch 23, Brooklyn, 1921-1964, 1965-
The Brooklyn branch, Patapsco Avenue and 3rd Street, opened October 15, 1921. The architect was Edward H. Glidden. The citizens of Brooklyn donated the land and Andrew Carnegie the dark brick North Italian-style building with tile roof and terra cotta-trimmed entrance. Pratt's annual report for 1921 said, "Branch 23's circulation far surpassed our expectation. In the first week it was nearly impossible to seat all who came to look and read." The branch saw heavier demands placed upon it during World War II as thousands of defense workers moved into Brooklyn, Curtis Bay and Fairfield. Patrons snapped up copies of "Modern Shipfitters Handbook" and "Modern Marine Pipefitting." Pamphlets on victory gardens were also popular.

The original Brooklyn branch closed April 9, 1964 and was demolished. Service was temporarily handled in a firehouse. A new Branch 23 opened August 30, 1965. Designed by Calvin Kern Kobsa, it is of light pink brick and dark olive steel trim. Mayor Theodore R. McKeldin dedicated the branch and said, "It is my wish that this library will always remain hospitable to any book that contains an idea. . . . The sober fact is that this library is either a portal to freedom, or it is nothing but a waste of money. Through these doors the citizen emerges into a wider, and greater and more wonderful world than he had inhabited before."

Branch 24, Irvington, 1924-1966
Branch 24, the Irvington branch, 214 South Loudon Avenue, near Massachusetts Avenue, opened January 31, 1924. Some $3,500 for the library site was raised by the Women's Club of Irvington, whose members conducted a house-to-house solicitation wherein residents "bought" bricks for their branch. The building was paid for partially from Andrew Carnegie funds and partially from a city appropriation. The building was designed by architect Thomas Machen. It closed September 28, 1961.

Branch 25, Roland Park, 1924-
Branch 25, Roland Avenue, Blackberry Lane and Longwood Road, was dedicated June 10, 1924. The architects were Buckler and Fenhagen. The land was donated by the Roland Park Civic League in April 1921. The city built the gray stone structure, for many years covered with ivy. The neighborhood developed a strong affection for the library. Even during the economically lean years of the 1930s, the branch received generous donations for its landscaping.

This branch was the subject of a heated historic preservation debate in 1965, when local architects and Roland Park residents argued before library officials against razing the branch, whose walls were constructed of 18-inch-thick gray stone. The residents declined to have a "ranch house" replacement branch built in their community.

When construction costs for a new branch proved too high, the 1924 building was remodeled. The original Gothic-style chandeliers, oak desks and a mural, the gift of artist Thomas C. Corner, were removed. The vaulted ceiling was covered by a false one. The remodeled library reopened for public use June 20, 1967.

Branch 26, Gardenville, 1926-
Branch 26, Belair Road and Quick Avenue, was dedicated March 27, 1926. The architect was Thomas Machen. In June 1924, Gardenville residents, the Belair Road Businessmen's Association and the Belair Road Improvement Association held a bazaar to raise funds for a library site. By July 30 of that year they presented the lot to the city, which then built structure. In 1946 librarian Ruth Staebner noted, "Most of the people are of German and Polish descent and they are predominantly Catholics. . . .They are interested in their homes, their children and their community. Their reading habits are the same that one finds in a small community practically everywhere. They want the lastest fiction and popular non-fiction, books that will tell them how to paint, redecorate or build a house, how to cook or plan a party and in the spring material on gardening is very much in demand. They are good readers. They ask for help in their book selection and appreciate any service that can be given them."

The Gardenville branch was enlarged and reopened May 18, 1959.

Branch 27, Westport, 1929-1961
Branch 27, the Westport branch, 2505 Annapolis Road, opened January 22, 1929. The architect was O. Eugene Adams. After World War II, new housing sprouted around Westport. With it came black library patrons. A branch annual report for 1946 said, " . . . interracial tension has increased (in the neighborhood, but) the library furnishes a neutral ground where members of both races can meet on terms of equality with a common interest. The best way to overcome prejudice is by 'getting to know the other fellow' and a genuine enthusiasm for books is helping our readers — negro and white —

317. The new bookmobile visits Belvedere and Park Heights avenues in 1949.

194

318. A Pratt mini-van delivers the latest books to Cherry Hill about 1969.

to bridge the barrier. The branch closed September 28, 1961 after the community it served had been disrupted and severed by a highway.

Branch 28, Edmondson Avenue, 1952-
Branch 28, the Edmondson Avenue Branch, was dedicated July 31, 1952 at Edmondson and Woodbridge avenues. The architects were Smith and Veale, who designed the structure to harmonize with the neighboring Edmondson Village Shopping Center.

Residents of the Edmondson Avenue area of West Baltimore had been campaigning for a branch library since the mid-1920s. There was considerable correspondence between City Hall and library officials, but little came of citizen demands for the branch.

In 1943 residents of the Edmondson-Rognel Heights area founded the Neighborhood Library Group and established a book lending station in an abandoned Welsh Construction Company sales office at Edmondson Avenue and Charing Cross Road. Led by Mrs. Donald G. Little, members of the Ten Hills, Westgate and Hunting Ridge community associations, Woman's Club of Ten Hills, Ten Hills Garden Club, School 232 Parent-Teacher Association and Women's Civic League backed the concept financially. Pratt supplied a part-time librarian and a basic collection of 800 books. The library moved in 1946 to a rent-free room in the recently completed Edmondson Village Shopping Center at 4508 Edmondson Avenue. It was open several days a week.

The citizen group continued to subsidize the library, with money and service, until 1950, Pratt assumed complete responsibility. Ground was broken for the permanent Branch 28 April 24, 1950. Its ground was donated by Jacob Meyerhoff, the developer of Edmondson Village Shopping Center. The library was one of three approved by a voters' referendum passed in 1947. Opening day was a tremendous success.

Branch 29, Herring Run, 1963-
Branch 29, the Herring Run Branch, opened at Erdman and Elmora avenues, February 25, 1963. The architects were Locke and Jackson. The one-story, brick building featured an outside glass-fronted exhibition case. The site was donated by Erdland Company, who developed real estate in Northeast Baltimore.

Branch 30, Dundalk, 1961-
Branch 30, Dundalk, Dundalk Avenue and Bushey Street, opened for public service October 3, 1961. The architects were Fenton and Lichtig. Mayor Harold Grady, Major General Henry C. Evans and Pratt Director Edwin Castagna spoke at the dedication services. The building's design involved glazed blue terra cotta panels. Vandals set fire to the branch May 23, 1981. The damage was estimated at $10,000.

Branch 31, Reisterstown Road, 1967-
Branch 31, the Reisterstown Road Branch, opened July 18, 1967 at Reisterstown Road and Kenshaw Avenue. The architects were Tatar and Kelly. It was constructed of "dark olive brick relieved by the bright white accents of the horizontal roof beams."

Pratt also maintains library centers to serve the needs of individual neighborhoods:

The Cherry Hill Center, 2490 Giles Road, opened June 7, 1976 in the Cherry Hill Multi-purpose Center. Library service to Cherry Hill began in late 1951 after experimental bookmobile service proved the need for a stationary book-lending unit. From 1951 to 1954 the book station was housed in a former construction shack, then moved to the former auditorium of the Cherry Hill Community Center on July 27, 1954 for two-day-a-week service.

Highlandtown Center, 3323 Eastern Avenue, opened January 16, 1975. Located on busy Eastern Avenue, the building once housed a Montgomery Ward catalog store. It is decorated with examples of the painted screens known so well throughout East Baltimore. "There is a strong sense of community in Highlandtown and the people view our center very much as theirs," wrote librarian Catherine Watson the year the center opened. Because of the multi-ethnic population of East Baltimore, the center has books in Polish, Greek, Ukranian, German, Italian, French and Spanish.

Kirk Avenue Center, located in the Kirk Avenue Multi-purpose Center, 909 East 22nd Street, opened September 15, 1971 and closed in July, 1984.

Lafayette Square Center, 1510 West Lafayette Avenue, opened January 17, 1974. Over the years, the staff have featured games, films, discussions, storytelling and music to appreciative patrons. A 1982 neighborhood fashion show packed the center to capacity. Librarian Ann Stepney recorded her impressions: "Many engaging and unique patrons have graced the center with their presence . . . The children who come in for daily hugs before going home.

Morrell Park Center, 2446 Washington Boulevard, opened August 17, 1973. The library is housed in a former dime store, once known as the Boulevard Variety. Patrons have told the staff how they, as children, frequented the store.

Reservoir Hill Center, 2001 Park Avenue, opened January 30, 1978. The center is housed in the old Bond mansion, an 18th Century home perched atop a small hill.

Washington Village Center, 906 Washington Boulevard, an adaptive reuse of a fire station, opened December 2, 1977.

Fort Worthington Center, 2710 E. Hoffman Street, opened January 12, 1976 and closed in July 1981.

INDEX

Artist Jack Lambert sketched Central patrons in 1926.

Credits: PHOTOGRAPHY

Author's collection: **24, 28-29, 32-33, 35-36, 42-44, 48, 50, 54-55, 57, 60-61, 64-66, 68, 73-74, 79-80, 84-85, 91, 93-94, 96, 97-100, 106-108, 110, 114-115, 117-118, 124-125, 127, 129-130, 132-134, 137-141, 148-150, 155-156, 159-160, 164-167, 171-176, 178, 180, 181-182, 187, 189, 191, 196-198, 201-202, 204, 208, 209-211, 213, 215, 217-218, 220-232-234, 236-237, 243, 245, 247, 248, 250-251, 253, 256-257, 259-260, 262-265, 267-269, 271-273, 275, 279-280, 282, 286-288, 290, 292-296, 300-302, 306, 308.**

Baltimore City Commission for Historic and Architectural Preservation: **72.**

Baltimore City Public Schools: **135, 185, 298.**

Baltimore County Public Library: **291, 304.**

Baltimore City Public Works Museum: **142.**

Chesapeake and Potomac Telephone Company: **235.**

Enoch Pratt Free Library: **2-5, 7-10, 12-20, 22, 25, 27, 31, 34, 51, 56, 59, 76, 82-83, 87, 101, 112, 119, 123, 126, 131, 143, 145, 151-153, 162, 179, 183-184, 186, 203, 212, 249, 255, 284, 289, 297, 299, 307, 310-316.**

Hagley Museum and Library, Wilmington: **192, 195**

The Maryland Historical Society: **62, 67, 71, 75, 77, 81, 121, 144, 147, 161, 169-170, 207, 303.**

The News American: **11, 21, 37, 63, 78, 86, 88, 109, 136, 146, 168, 193, 200, 261, 281.**

Peale Museum: **1, 6, 9, 30, 39, 40-41, 45-47, 69-70, 89, 95, 102-105, 111, 116, 120, 128, 154, 157-158, 163, 177, 190, 214, 219, 231, 238-240, 244, 246, 252, 254, 252, 254, 258, 274, 276-277, 305, 309.**

Private collections: Allan Czarnowsky **241-242;** A. Michael Isekoff: **199;** June Kerr: **205-206;** Emma Mitchell, **278;** Eleanor Pape: **270;** Frederick Schwedes Jr: **23;** George Voith: **92, 216, 285.**

Smithsonian: **38.**

University of Maryland, Baltimore County, Albin O. Kuhn Library and Gallery, Edward L. Bafford Photography Collection: **26, 49, 53, 122, 188, 194, 266.**

319. Shoppers converged on Howard and Lexington streets, the retailing crossroads of Baltimore in 1928, when this photo was made. Within steps of this intersection were Hochschild, Kohn & Company, Hutzler Brothers, Stewart & Company, Brager's, Eisenberg's, the May Company, a Read's drug store, Joel Gutman Company and Julius Gutman Company. O'Neill & Company was east of this spot, at Charles and Lexington streets, as was The Hub, at Charles and Baltimore streets.

Credits: ILLUSTRATIONS

Edwin Tunis, the artist who drew many maps and illustrations for the Pratt Library over the years, designed the maps on pages iv-v and 186 and the endpapers used in this book. An historical and literary map he designed for the Pratt in 1931 has sold more than 15,000 copies. The endpapers reproduced in this book were originally used at Pratt's book bindery as volumes needed rebinding. Tunis also wrote and illustrated number of books.

Newspaper artist Jack Lambert, who had a long career at Baltimore newspapers, drew the illustration of patrons at the old Central Library on page 196.

320. A graceful screen atop the Central Pratt Children's Department entrance.

ABOUT THE AUTHOR

Jacques Kelly was born in Baltimore and discovered the Pratt Central's Maryland Department, its books, files and photographs as soon as he was old enough to spend Saturdays downtown. He researched his three previous publications there: "Peabody Heights to Charles Village," (1976), "Bygone Baltimore" (1982) and "Maryland, An Historical Portrait, The First 350 Years" (1983). He is a graduate of the Baltimore Academy of the Visitation, Loyola High School and the Catholic University of America. After joining the staff of The News American in 1972 and serving as a feature writer and reporter, he became a local columnist and editorial writer. He lives in Charles Village, just up the street from Pratt's Branch 6.

Designed by Sandra R. Sparks

The text is set in Times Roman. The display type face is Garamond Bold. Printed by the Walsworth Publishing Company.